ADVENTURES WITH OLD HOUSES

ADVENTURES WITH OLD HOUSES

By

RICHARD HAMPTON JENRETTE

Foreword by

HRH THE PRINCE OF WALES

Principal Photography by John M. Hall

WYRICK & COMPANY

Charleston

Published by Wyrick & Company
1-A Pinckney Street
Charleston, SC 29401

Creative Direction: Paul Waner   Design: Don Giordano

Printed and bound in Hong Kong by Palace Press International

Library of Congress Cataloging-in-Publication Data

Jenrette, Richard H.
    Adventures with old houses / Richard Hampton Jenrette ; foreword by HRH The Prince
of Wales ; principal photography by John M. Hall.
        p. cm.
    Includes index.
    ISBN 0-941711-46-3
    1. Architecture, Domestic--United States--Conservation and restoration. 2. Historic
buildings--United States--Conservation and restoration. 3. Neoclassicism
(Architecture)--United States. 4. Furniture--United States--History--19th century. I.
Title.

NA7207 .J45 2000
728'.37'0973028--dc21   99-045641

Contents

HRH THE PRINCE OF WALES

HRH The Prince of Wales with Richard H. Jenrette
at the Roper House in Charleston, South Carolina.

I first met Dick Jenrette in 1989 when he very generously offered me the use of his splendid Greek Revival mansion while I was in Charleston, South Carolina, for several days attending a conference for business people. What neither of us realised when I accepted his invitation was that Hurricane Hugo would make a devastating visit to Charleston a few weeks prior to my arrival. Mr. Jenrette's home overlooks Charleston harbour and the direct hit of the eye of the storm brought five feet of water into the first floor of the mansion and totally washed away the adjoining gardens.

Yet all was polished and serene by the time of my arrival.... Neither the necessity to repaint and rewire the entire first floor and replant the gardens, nor the time constraints could deter Mr. Jenrette from extending the gracious Southern hospitality for which Charleston is famed.

The Roper House, which takes its name from its builder in 1838, displays not only Mr. Jenrette's commitment to preserving the best of America's architectural heritage, but also his extraordinary collection of classical American art, antiques and other furnishings.

When I recognized several paintings in the house by the late Felix Kelly, whose work I admire and whose help I had sought in the past, of other early 19th Century houses in America, I learned that Roper House was only one of several great classical houses owned and restored by Mr. Jenrette. I understand that the total has now reached seven, not including others he has had a hand in restoring through various preservation groups in America. No wonder some of his admirers have described Dick as a one-person National Trust for Historic Preservation.

Since then I was pleased to learn that Dick has received the coveted Louise duPont Crowninshield Award, presented by the National Trust for his outstanding contribution to preserving America's architectural heritage. I was even more pleased to see that the Hadrian Award, which was presented to me by the World Monuments Fund several years ago, was awarded to Dick this past year.

Dick Jenrette's passion for classical architecture, and in sharing it with others, parallels my own interests in that and other forms of architecture in Britain and elsewhere. This book represents a fascinating personal memoir of how one person, while building several highly successful businesses, also found a fulfilling hobby in protecting and preserving his nation's architectural heritage. I hope the publication of this book will serve as an inspiration and guide to others to follow in his footsteps.

ACKNOWLEDGEMENTS

Given the subject of this book—restoring beautiful old houses—my first acknowledgement goes to the long-deceased owners and builders of these great old houses that have stood the test of time. They had a vision of beauty and an optimism to build for the ages as the fledgling United States entered the nineteenth century. You will be reading about all of them: the Livingstons of New York; the Donaldsons of both New York and North Carolina; the Kirklands of North Carolina; the Ropers, Mannings, and Hamptons of South Carolina; the McEvoys in the West Indies; and, in the twentieth century, the George F. Bakers of New York. In living in their homes, I feel I have come to learn a great deal about their lives. I am not a very spiritual person, but if I were, I could easily believe they are still keeping watch over their beloved homesteads. I am nothing more than a caretaker and feel grateful for the years I have been given to watch over and enjoy these beautiful places, preserving them for the future as part of America's architectural heritage.

And I certainly didn't do it alone—either in finding these houses, restoring them, furnishing them and, more recently, completing this book about my experiences. Bill Thompson has played a key role in finding, restoring, and decorating all these houses. Margize Howell and Kathy Healy have been constantly helpful in researching, documenting, and helping me keep track of the thousands of objects now in the collection of antiques and fine arts that fill these houses. Jack Smith, for more than twenty years, has been my right-hand man in watching over the physical condition of all these properties, aided by a loyal and talented group of site managers: Ernie Townsend, Bill and David Crowther and Louis Hall. They, in turn, have been backed by many dedicated helpers.

Without the help of Maria Fitzsimmons, my ever-patient, energetic and talented secretary, I never could possibly have had time for such a time-consuming hobby as restoring old houses, while at the same time helping restore DLJ in the difficult 1970s and Equitable in the early 1990s. Maria also had the unenviable task of translating my virtually indecipherable handwriting into this book. She jokes that her job security comes from being the only person able to read my handwriting and the only person who can understand my French, when I try to speak it. Maria need never worry about job security because she is indispensable, in every way. I do want to say thanks also to others at my office who have been of invaluable help over the years, especially Joe Hillis and Mike Carew, both recently retired, and Emma Romano, now just married.

To all of these many wonderful people, as well as others who have helped in so many ways but are not mentioned, I give heartfelt thanks. I am also grateful to my business partners and associates over the years who have indulged my love of antiquity—and many times have become similarly addicted. I love you all and I am eternally grateful for your friendship and support.

My final acknowledgement is to "acknowledge" that, "Yes, Virginia, I did write this book all by myself" (by hand, as Maria will attest). If you don't like the writing, I'm sure you will love the beautiful photography by John Hall and the creative direction for the book provided by Paul Waner. Both have been invaluable partners, and I am so thankful for all their support and the talent they brought to bear on this project. I especially want to thank Connie and Pete Wyrick, my publishers at Wyrick & Company in Charleston, who share my love of old houses. They read my manuscript, probably decided it was too wordy but nevertheless wanted to publish it because—for better or worse—it's the way I am. "I go with the houses," which is what I told another publisher who liked the idea of a book on my houses, but wanted to use another writer. Thanks Connie and Pete—I think you're terrific!

Richard Hampton Jenrette

CHAPTER 1

CONFESSIONS OF A "HOUSE-AHOLIC"

Restoring fine old homes to their former glory has been a hobby—some say a passion—of mine for the past thirty years. A *disease* might be a more accurate description! Friends have described me as a "house-aholic" who can't say no to a fine old house that has fallen on hard times.

It is certainly true that I seem to have an affinity for endangered old houses; they seem to seek me out. Currently I own six historic properties, most of them dating back to the early nineteenth century. But this is just the tip of the iceberg. I've owned and restored eight other old houses and rebuilt an antebellum hotel, all of which I later sold or gave away. Through involvement in various preservation groups, I've also had a hand in rescuing dozens of other old houses from possible destruction or ruination. No wonder people say I'm addicted to old houses.

None of my houses was acquired as a result of a conscious, planned decision to go out and buy a home. I guess you could call these acquisitions "impulse purchases." I just stumbled on to them and each was irresistible. Even though I may not have had the money

The author at Edgewater, Barrytown, N.Y.

We all know that if you go out looking for your dream house, you cannot find it. You make compromises. If your need is urgent, often you overpay.

in the bank, at the time, I somehow always found a way to come up with the requisite funds. Where there is a will, there is a way.

Buying a house in such a seemingly helter-skelter manner is not as stupid as it sounds at first blush. We all know that if you go out looking for your dream house, you cannot find it. You make compromises. If your need is urgent, often you overpay. In contrast, each of my purchases was made when I really didn't need another house. The uniqueness of the property and its architectural distinction had to be overwhelmingly compelling to capture my interest and overcome the logic of not buying. And because in each case I really didn't have to buy the house, I was able to bargain and secure a low purchase price, or so it seems with hindsight.

One thing leads to another, and possession of these fine old early American houses led to the next logical step—collecting antiques of the period of the houses to furnish them. While I started out with mostly English antiques, somewhere along the way I decided to concentrate on American furniture of the early nineteenth century, the period in which most of the six houses were built. After all, these were American houses, and American antiques somehow seemed more at home in them. Today I own literally thousands of antiques, almost entirely American in origin (more specifically, New York) from the early nineteenth century, as well as related art objects: portraits, landscape paintings, urns, clocks, carpets, chandeliers, porcelain dinner services; you name it, I've collected it. Many of the latter *objets d'art* are European in origin since U.S. manufactures at the time rarely extended to these luxury items.

Along the way I also transmitted this love of architecture, art and antiques to the two business enterprises that I have headed—the investment banking firm of Donaldson, Lufkin & Jenrette, Inc. and The Equitable Life Assurance Society. Both have handsome public spaces filled with interesting and valuable Americana, which has appreciated significantly in value over the years, unlike the usual banal office trappings which often decline in value as soon as purchased. Even more satisfying, I have observed that many officers and employees of DLJ and Equitable, as well as other clients and friends, seem to have caught my old house and antiques fever. Many have bought and restored old houses and have begun to collect antiques. This hobby is definitely contagious!

By referring to this house and antique collecting and restoration hobby as a "disease" or an "addiction," I am probably doing a disservice to my real purpose in writing this book, which is to share with you some of the joys and rewards that can come with this fascinating hobby and encourage you to join in the fun. It's never too late. There are always bargains to be found in old houses and antiques.

Don't be turned off if this hobby sounds horribly expensive. It can be, but it need not be. You obviously don't need to own six houses filled with antiques, as I do now after a life-time of collecting. In fact, it's far better to start slowly, feeling your way along as your knowledge and income hopefully increase over the years. I started out in a small way, literally on a shoestring, borrowing most of the purchase price of my first old house. Most of the antiques were acquired, one at a time, over long periods of time at what now seem like bargain prices— although they didn't seem so at the time. I stretched and squirmed and bargained on each purchase, which I might not have done had I been more affluent at the time I began collecting. Today those acquisition prices look very cheap. The reality is that investing in fine old houses and antiques can be tremendously rewarding financially over periods of time. It's one of the few situations in life where *time is on your side*; the older things get, the better (and more valuable).

While most people who put their money in the stock market fifteen years ago have done spectacularly well, my old houses and antiques appear to have appreciated just as much in value, judging by the sale of comparable properties or the prices at Sotheby's and Christie's or in the dealers' shops. And I've had a lot more fun with them than a portfolio of stocks (even when they go up in value!). Obviously, if hard times return—like another Depression such as we had in the 1930s (and which I am old enough to remember)—my houses could turn back into white elephants and the antiques would lose a lot of their value. But that would also be the case with most common stocks.

While I am not recommending that you go out and buy an old house or a piece of antique furniture simply as an investment, the good news is that they do tend to keep their value and appreciate with age. The more unusual or unique or limited in supply, the better in terms of long-term appreciation. But in buying an old house or an antique, your primary motivation should be your own enjoyment and the satisfaction that you get out of ownership. If it also turns out to be a good investment, so much the better.

The satisfaction of owning something old and beautiful can be heightened if you've had a hand in restoring its former glory—as opposed to buying a house or piece of furniture already in pristine condition. Much of the fun comes from seeing something that was once beautiful returned to its original elegance. My restoration efforts have, of necessity, been limited to finding and hiring skilled artisans who could perform the work of restoring the house or the antique furniture I picked up along the way. I've been too busy to do it myself, nor do I have the requisite skills. But, by becoming intricately involved in the restoration process, I think I have made some contribution beyond just paying the bills.

Finding the skills needed to do a proper restoration job can be a challenging assignment but is not impossible today. The good news is that the number of skilled artisans seems to have taken a quantum leap in the last twenty years or so since I've been collecting old houses and antiques. Few in my generation seemed to have the arts and crafts mentality or patience needed for restoration. Starting in the late 1960s, young people—perhaps alienated by business or the Vietnam War—rediscovered some of the ancient handicrafts related to the creation and repair of beautiful objects. These skills include carving, polishing, gilding, marbleizing and other *trompe l'oeil* painting, as well as basic construction skills like plastering and masonry—done the old-

My first purchase was Roper House, built in 1838, overlooking the harbor of Charleston, S.C. The $100,000 purchase price in 1968 seems like a great bargain in retrospect.

fashioned way, to last. The bad news, of course, is that really good restoration doesn't come cheaply. But what a difference it can make when done right.

Discovering and encouraging some of this restoration talent that is available today has been lots of fun. I have gained a whole new set of friends in a world apart from Wall Street or Main Street. I also take pleasure in having helped many of these talented individuals in advancing their careers as artists in their field of restoration expertise. In this respect, praise, where justified, is even more important than the almighty dollar. Most of these skilled artisans aren't in restoration just for the money. They are turned on by creating beauty. If you recognize and appreciate their accomplishments, they'll work miracles for you.

CHAPTER 2

HOW I GOT HOOKED
ON OLD HOUSES

How did I get so addicted to old houses or, more specifically, restoring old houses? That is a question I've been asked over and over by people who have visited my houses. My glib answer, which usually seems to suffice, is that I saw *Gone With the Wind* about a dozen too many times as a kid growing up in Raleigh, North Carolina. It's actually true. The movie came out in 1939, when I was ten years of age. It came at a time when we were all poor in the South, and visions of the great mansions and grandeur of a former era certainly made an indelible impression. The past seemed better than the present. Scarlett O'Hara was driven to restore Tara, her ancestral home, to its former glory after the destruction of the Civil War. There is no denying *GWTW* had an impact on me— along with a lot of other Americans, judging by the proliferation of houses with white columns that ensued.

But even before I saw *GWTW*, I can recall drawing pictures of imaginary houses from about age six or

Visions of the great mansions and grandeur of a former era certainly made an indelible impression. The past seemed better than the present.

When I first became interested in architecture, I never dreamed that I would end up owning anything so grand as Millford Plantation (circa 1840) in South Carolina.

seven on. Everyone said I would grow up to be an architect, though that idea never distinctly appealed to me. I just liked to draw, and I liked houses. You could create your own fantasy castle with pencil or crayon. In a similar vein, I recall rushing out to the sandy driveway behind our house after it rained and shaping rivers and canals and whole cities out of sand. So it's not surprising that I still love building things or restoring them today.

I also distinctly remember taking an active role at age five when my parents were looking to buy a new house. That was 1934, in the depths of the Depression, and so there were lots of nice houses for sale at bargain prices. My father, an insurance salesman, must have made some good sales for us to be able to afford a new house at that time. I remember having very strong opinions, even at that young age, as to which house we should buy. As things turned out, none of the houses I favored was chosen by my parents—my first lesson that I would have to do it "my way" in the future if I were ever to be satisfied. The house that Mother and Dad eventually chose wasn't bad— sort of a simplified 1920s Tudor style that was popular at the time— but it lacked any real architectural distinction. It could never have passed for Tara or Twelve Oaks.

There was, however, an unexpected consolation prize that accrued to me from living in the house on Fairview Road that my parents selected. Around the corner from our house —a few blocks away on Oberlin Road—there began to rise out of a vast empty field what was absolutely the most magnificent house I (or anyone in Raleigh) had ever seen. This was the future Tatton Hall, a magnificent Palladian pile built by Mr. N.E. Edgerton, who clearly had survived the Depression in good financial order. Many years later on a trip to England I discovered the original Tatton Hall, which I learned was the ancestral home of the Egerton (spelled without a *d*) family in Britain. Mr. Edgerton must have heard about it or visited it somewhere along the line, as clearly he was inspired to build a monument of sorts to his family's ancestral home. The American Tatton Hall is, if anything, grander than its British antecedent.

On long summer evenings after dinner, my mother, sister, and I used to take walks up Oberlin Road to watch Tatton Hall rising out of the ground. It took a year or two to build. The house faced due west so we could see right through it, beautifully silhouetted against the sunset. Raleigh had never seen anything like Tatton Hall and that is still true sixty years later. It is probably the finest piece of classical architecture ever built in North Carolina, including Tryon Palace (the British colonial governor's palace in New Bern) and some of the great antebellum mansions. Only Biltmore, the Vanderbilt mansion in Asheville, exceeds it in opulence. Watching the construction of Tatton Hall was a great thrill and inspiration to me and it must have fostered in me a desire to have something grand myself one day—though my aspirations then most certainly were for something far more modest than a Tatton Hall.

While my hometown of Raleigh never was known especially for great classical architecture, unlike Charleston or Philadelphia or tidewater Virginia, I certainly made the most of what was there as a kid. On Sunday drives and walks, I would always coax my parents to go by my favorite houses. I tended to favor houses with columns, of which there were quite a few— both pre-Civil War, late-nineteenth-century classical revival and more modern post-*GWTW* versions.

Some years later in college at the University of North Carolina, I joined the Chi Psi fraternity. Unhappily for me, Chi Psi didn't have columns on its house, and I used to envy the Dekes and the Betas as well as some of the other houses with grand colonnaded porticos where the brothers sat and leisurely sipped cocktails. But Chi Psi Lodge, as our house was quaintly called, was an imposing structure, sitting on the highest point in Chapel Hill—by far the largest house and grounds of any fraternity, even if it lacked columns. It was vaguely French provincial in architecture and afforded myriad opportunities to experiment with interior decorating and landscaping its beautiful, oak-shaded three-acre lot. Chi Psi became sort of a laboratory for me in trying out ideas on decorating and landscaping that I came across. During my period there, the alumni also added a large new wing to the Lodge. This extensive construction further whet my appetite for building projects. I never minded all the sawdust and inconvenience. It was fun seeing things built.

The University of North Carolina had many magnificent buildings with massive colonnades which never failed to stir my imagination and certainly shaped my architectural tastes. I especially liked the magnificent Corinthian-columned library (now called Wilson Library) at the foot of the campus mall. I used

to go there each night to study. It became a second home of sorts. Nearby Duke University had beautiful Gothic architecture, but Duke was "the enemy" then (now I am a trustee of the Duke Endowment and love Duke)—perhaps one of the reasons it took me another thirty years to develop a taste for Gothic. I also enjoyed football weekends at the University of Virginia, which gave me the opportunity to soak up some of Mr. Jefferson's classical architectural ideas along with UVA booze. Whenever I went to Charlottesville, I would always make the pilgrimage to Monticello, Jefferson's inspiring mountaintop home. The Jefferson-designed University of Virginia campus,

A side view of Millford, which may help explain why "The past seemed better than the present" when I was growing up during the Depression of the 1930s.

called The Lawn, also impressed me, as did the fraternity houses along Rugby Road.

As I look back over my exposure to grand architecture in elementary and high school as well as college days, I can't keep from contrasting this experience with the dreary non-architecture that today's school kids face. Both Hayes-Barton elementary school and Broughton High School in Raleigh were

architectural jewels in their own way. Some of Thomas Jefferson's views that the architecture of the school should be part of the educational process evidently were still in vogue in America through the 1920s and 1930s when these schools were built. In stark contrast, many of today's elementary and high schools look to me like factories—long, unadorned flat-topped buildings devoid of any architectural ornamentation. Yes, they are air-conditioned and wired for the Internet, but I feel these students are deprived—starved for beauty and good architecture, even though they may not realize it. No wonder students (and probably teachers also) seem to feel no loyalty to these bland and faceless schools, which in some communities don't even have names (instead, P.S. 38). I can understand why no one would want to have one of those boring, nondescript buildings named in their honor.

I guess my final architectural lessons came from Harvard University, where I attended the Graduate Business School. The Harvard Business School's neo-Georgian style campus was built in the 1920s with funds provided by Mr. George Fisher Baker, one of the great bankers of his time. Years later I bought Mr. Baker's elegant Georgian town house in New York City, which I still own. Mr. Baker, who was keenly interested in architecture, took an active role in the business school's

Thirty years after graduating from Harvard Business School, I purchased this New York town house built for banker George Fisher Baker, donor of the handsome campus occupied by the Business School, which influenced my architectural taste—as well as my views on business management.

construction. McKim, Mead & White, one of New York's most highly regarded architectural firms at the time, were the architects. The school was built all of a piece at one time, and it is magnificent. Without doubt, going to school and living in these splendid buildings at Harvard—even though they were only replicas of an earlier period—shaped the direction of my architectural tastes. Just being in Boston with access to the entire city's and region's vast cornucopia of good architecture was an inspiration to me.

On spring recess from Harvard, I also visited the imposing South Carolina home of one of my classmates, Charlie Coker. It evidently suited my new taste for grandeur. Joan Coker, now Charlie's wife, recalls my saying to her, "One day I'm going to have a house just like this!" Joan must have had the same idea since she married Charlie and lives in that same house today.

When I subsequently took a job in New York at Brown Brothers Harriman & Co., a private bank dating back to 1818, my tastes were fixed—probably forever—on the classical mode of architecture. Brown Brothers was entered through a sweeping staircase in a handsome domed rotunda. The partners labored in a high-ceilinged, oak-paneled chamber with a large coal-burning fireplace at one end, portraits of the founders, and large roll-top desks. I decided that this rather nineteenth-century Dickensian look was for me. I always had difficulty relating to the stark, modernist architecture which was taking over American cities at that time, functional though it might be. Today I find that most of those glass and concrete, flat-topped buildings that were considered *de rigueur* and so terribly modern in the 1960s already look dated and out of fashion. Classical architectural details have returned to today's post-modern architecture.

CHAPTER 3

ON MY OWN
(EARLY INFLUENCES)

When I moved to New York to work at Brown Brothers Harriman, I shared an apartment with A. Jones Yorke IV, a fellow North Carolinian who also had been a classmate and good friend at Harvard Business School. I was fortunate in my choice of a roommate, especially since Jones' mother, Martha Best Yorke—the quintessential southern grande dame—took me under her wing. Mrs. Yorke sent up a truckload of English antiques, oriental carpets, and Audubon prints from her beautiful home in North Carolina that made our otherwise undistinguished New York apartment the envy of all our friends. Under Mrs. Yorke's direction, I purchased my first antique—an English burled walnut chest-on-chest. That got me started on a collecting career that still continues unabated. Mrs. Yorke and her husband, who was retired, were both so interested in art, antiques, and decorating that I just assumed this was the way of all civilized people. Mrs. Yorke certainly pointed me

After I had made a few fumbling efforts at self-decorating, Macon Patton, one of my colleagues at DLJ, convinced me to call Otto Zenke.

I stumbled upon Edgewater, shimmering in the late afternoon sunlight reflected off the Hudson River, in 1969. It was love at first sight and made me forget my plans to build a glass house.

in the way of beauty, though my interests already lay in this direction.

My roommate got married a year later, and there went the English antiques. But after a couple more apartment-sharing arrangements, my ship finally came in financially, so to speak, several years after we had started Donaldson, Lufkin & Jenrette. At last I was able to afford that luxury of New York luxuries, a "co-op" apartment. I found a beautiful maisonette at 455 East 57th Street, the first piece of real estate I ever owned, though technically with a co-op you don't really own a specific apartment but rather you receive stock in the building corporation and a lease on a specific apartment. Never mind such technicalities; I finally felt myself king of my own domain—a New York co-op that was all mine!

After I had made a few fumbling efforts at self-decorating, Macon Patton, one of my colleagues at DLJ and also a native North Carolinian, convinced me to call Otto Zenke, then the reigning interior decorator in North Carolina. This turned out to be an inspired decision. Zenke, a confirmed Anglophile, specialized in late Georgian and Regency English furniture and interiors, encompassing the late eighteenth and early nineteenth centuries. Otto took me in tow, bombarding me with books on Georgian architecture and furnishings. In addition to his Greensboro, North Carolina shop, he had his own antique dealership in London, which I visited several times. On those occasions, Otto would drive me into the countryside to visit the best of British country home architecture. He was truly knowledgeable on the subject and his tastes in decorating were excellent—very understated, very "smooth" (his favorite word to describe rooms that flowed seamlessly from one to the other). Forty years later, I still like decorating that is "smooth."

In record time, Otto had equipped my New York maisonette with all the accoutrements that one could possibly desire. He installed a handsome antique Georgian fireplace mantel as a focal point and had his carpenter build pilasters and moldings to define the architecture of the room. Then one day a huge moving van from North Carolina arrived at my door, and by the end of the day, beautifully cut draperies and carpets had been installed, chandeliers hung, antique as well as comfortable upholstered furniture installed, old leather-bound books placed in the bookcases, dining room porcelain service in place—everything I could possibly need. It was what we later began to call "Instant Otto." As a final touch, Otto Zenke said, "Now you will need some help to take care of it all." He produced Jack and Thelma, an aging but distinguished-looking couple that had previously worked with Otto. Jack served as my part-time butler when I had parties. Thelma came in regularly to clean. Otto was not about to let me mess up his masterpiece.

And it was a masterpiece of sorts, a jewel-like setting that subsequently appeared in several magazines. The look that Otto Zenke favored still sticks with me today. The centerpiece of his rooms inevitably would be a handsome Georgian fireplace. On either side of the mantel he favored tall bookcases, filled with old leather-bound books. Sofas and comfortable chairs with lamps would be placed on either side of the fireplace. The resulting warm, home-like feeling of mellow leather book bindings and beautiful architecture and a cheery fire in the fireplace is one that I have replicated over and over in my other houses over the years. A house is not a home to me without a library or drawing room with a handsome fireplace mantel and bookcases filled with old leather-bound books. Those old books, by the way, have also skyrocketed in price, and are probably among my best investments. Otto used to "buy them by the yard" back in the 1950s when they could be bought in quantity for $1 apiece. Today most would go for $50 or more. The craftsmanship of some is extraordinary.

The maisonette at 455 East 57th Street was not Otto Zenke's only work for me. I sold that apartment a few years later and moved to Brussels to help our firm establish a European presence. The logistics of Brussels didn't faze Otto Zenke one bit. It was still "Instant Otto" shortly after I had rented an eighteenth-century farmhouse in Waterloo, outside Brussels (the house overlooked the site of the Battle of Waterloo). Working out of his London office, Otto gave me a stylishly decorated "farmhouse" almost overnight. It may have looked more like North Carolina than Belgium, but I was pleased with the result.

Otto Zenke, who was twenty-five years or so older than I, died many years ago, but his legacy of good taste still lingers, especially in the two Carolinas. In his day, he decorated the finest homes of North Carolina as well as some in South Carolina. Many stand surprisingly unchanged today, monuments to his timeless classical interiors. Undoubtedly he raised the taste level of countless Carolinians. He is still fondly remembered there. Knowing him and being his client was a great experience for me at a formative period in my life. Too bad no one ever did a book on his work. At heart, he was probably more architect than designer, and he used his knowledge of Georgian architecture to good effect in designing handsome interior spaces.

But times change and people change. Otto Zenke was fighting valiantly against the post-World War II Bauhaus modernism and minimalism in architecture and decorating that was so *à la mode*. By the late 1960s, his English Georgian look was considered by many to be *passé*. While I never could warm up to these modern, minimalist trends, I did worry that perhaps Otto might be too rigid in sticking so religiously to the English Georgian look, admitting no other nationalities or periods or new ideas. In Brussels, I had been impressed by the extraordinary art-filled all glass apartment of Baron Leon Lambert, who lived like a Medici banker on the top floor of his family-controlled Banque Lambert, lodged in a sleek new Skidmore, Owings & Merrill-designed structure. Even I, with my traditional tastes, had to admit Leon's apartment was spectacular—high-ceilinged rooms filled with the best impressionist and contemporary art, set off by stark white walls and dramatic lighting. It made my farmhouse outside Brussels look very old-fashioned. As one of the founders of a thoroughly modern Wall Street firm I began to wonder if I might need a look in my residence that was somewhat more eclectic, proving that I too was an *homme du monde*.

Back in New York I was still so impressed by Baron Lambert's stunning apartment that I commissioned one of his favorite architects, Ed Knowles, to design a weekend home for me in Hunterdon County, New Jersey, on a steep hillside overlooking the Delaware River. It was to be a series of three high-ceilinged cubes: mostly glass, with connecting terraces and a "drop-dead view" down the river to the distant Delaware Water Gap. It would have been spectacular in that setting. Had I built this all-glass, modern home, it might have ended my love affair with old houses.

Before I could begin construction, I stumbled, quite by accident, on Edgewater, a marvelous circa 1820 Palladian villa located on the Hudson River about ninety miles upriver from New York. When I saw this mellow old building with its six tall Doric columns shimmering in the late afternoon sunlight reflected off the river on a beautiful fall day in 1969, it was love at first sight. I knew that the house belonged to the author Gore Vidal, but I did not know him at the time, nor that the house was for sale. What I did know was that Edgewater had suddenly made me forget the glass house I proposed to build in New Jersey.

Upon returning to New York that evening, I received a telephone call from Anthony Hail, a San Francisco designer who was doing some work for me in New York. Tony said he had just been to Rome where he had visited Gore Vidal, who told him he planned to sell Edgewater, his house on the Hudson. Hail, who had visited the house, said, "It's to die over" (one of his favorite expressions) and "You have got to buy it." I replied that by some strange coincidence I had just seen the house that very day and loved it. Three days later I had concluded a transatlantic deal with Gore Vidal to buy it, practically sight unseen.

Let me tell you a bit about Anthony Hail and his very considerable influence on my still evolving taste in

art and architecture. I met Tony through Lou Walker, a Harvard Business School classmate of mine living in San Francisco. At the time, Hail was the reigning interior designer in the City by the Bay. He had a glittering, jewel-like setting on top of Telegraph Hill. A transplanted southerner from Nashville, Tennessee, who also had lived abroad for many years before settling in San Francisco, Tony Hail seemed the answer to my desire for a somewhat more eclectic look—one that respected the past but seemed fresher and more up-to-date than Otto Zenke's more formal Georgian settings.

Tony was particularly adept at mixing elements from different periods and different cultures. His southern background made him a traditionalist at heart, but his years in Europe had given him a more cosmopolitan taste for eighteenth-century French and especially classical Swedish, Danish and Russian furniture and *objets d'art*. Tony's years of residence in San Francisco also led him to mix-in oriental furnishings, such as a fabulous twelve-panel coromandel screen that he found for me which I later stupidly sold. Tony believed that beautiful Chinese things fit in with any period or décor, a view to which I still subscribe.

In the rooms Tony Hail decorated for his clients, all those global antiquities were mixed and presented against a bland or neutral background palette: off-white walls or very light pastel colors (he always emphasized "clear colors"—no muddy or umber colors for him). He frequently used beige wall-to-wall carpets, with the monotony broken up by faded but beautiful oriental rugs, which he placed on top of the contemporary beige carpets at strategic points. Tony was rather restrained in his use of color, or so it seemed to me. Perhaps he felt strong colors competed too much with the elegant

furnishings he prescribed for his clients. Tony himself had been greatly influenced by the work of the legendary Billy Baldwin, then the *beau ideal* of fashionable New York society decorators, and David Hicks, the most aristocratic of British designers. At the time, both combined classical antiques and *objets d'art* with stylish contemporary designs for carpets and fabrics. The resulting eclectic melange seemed timeless as well as contemporary. It was just what I wanted at this stage of my life.

Added to Tony Hail's skills as a decorator was a delicious if sometimes mischievous sense of humor. It was always great fun to be around him. The best article on Tony Hail's career, and the influences that shaped him, is Sarah Medford's "Hail Fellow Well Met" which appeared in the November 1996 issue of *Town & Country*. Someone should do a book on Hail's long and successful career as a designer.

Edgewater (near center, above) has been the great love of my life, nestled on a peninsula into the Hudson River. To the left is the new guesthouse and to the right is the new pool house.

Tony Hail, even more than Leon Lambert, got me out of the rut of thinking that everything had to be late-eighteenth-century English Georgian. Before I knew it Tony had me buying French Louis XVI mantels, Swedish and Danish chairs, Russian chandeliers and lots of oriental *objets d'art*. Eclectic was in, as far as I was concerned in this period of my life. It seemed a happy compromise between the strict modernism favored by Baron Lambert and the out-of-favor traditionalists like Otto Zenke.

CHAPTER 4

DAYS OF EMPIRE
(THE LATE 1960s)

Tony Hail came into my life at a prosperous time when I had lots of projects requiring the services of an interior designer. The 1960s were years of great prosperity on Wall Street and nowhere more so than in our firm, Donaldson, Lufkin & Jenrette, Inc., which I had co-founded in 1960 along with Bill Donaldson and Dan Lufkin, two Harvard Business School classmates. DLJ was the hottest firm on Wall Street in the 1960s (it still seems to be red hot in the late 1990s). We capped this first decade of rapid growth by taking the company public in early 1970, making DLJ the first New York Stock Exchange firm to sell its own shares to the public. For the first time in my life I felt I had the financial resources to indulge my growing appetite for old houses and antiques.

"Indulge" is certainly the right word. I embarked on an unplanned buying spree of old houses, including an old hotel. Perhaps it was a case of my newfound wealth (it really wasn't all that much in retrospect) burning a hole in my pocket. But I did stumble on some absolutely

I came across the Roper House by accident while visiting clients in Charleston.

My first purchase, in 1968, was the Robert William Roper House, a splendid colonnaded Greek Revival mansion built in 1838 and located on the "High Battery" overlooking the historic harbor of Charleston, South Carolina.

magnificent old houses at bargain prices. I could not resist them.

My first purchase, in 1968, was the Robert William Roper House, a splendid colonnaded Greek Revival mansion built in 1838 and located on the "High Battery" overlooking the historic harbor of Charleston, South Carolina. I came across this imposing mansion by accident, while visiting Charles and Carol Duell, who owned another splendid antebellum mansion a few doors away. After a moonlight walking tour of historic Charleston I remarked—rather tastelessly, since I was a guest in the Duells' house, one of the handsomest in town—that my favorite house in Charleston was 9 East Battery (the Roper House). Instead of being offended, Charlie remarked, "It just might be for sale."

The next day he introduced me to Drayton Hastie, the owner, and I learned that the house of my *Gone With The Wind*-influenced dreams was indeed for sale. But there was one caveat. Drayton's 76-year-old mother, Mrs. C. Norwood Hastie, would have to be granted a life tenancy on the principal floor, the *piano nobile*, which in Charleston is always on the second floor. That suited me just fine since I was fully engaged in New York and certainly did not need a big house in Charleston. It also

The Mills House, my one venture as a hotelier, included an elegant cocktail lounge by John Dickinson. The trompe l'oeil carpet resembles old brick.

made the price cheaper and allowed me to structure an arrangement where I had to put up only half the $100,000 purchase price as long as Mrs. Hastie lived there. Incidentally, after I bought the house, which seemed like a great bargain to me coming from New York, I was told by a local, "Dick, don't you realize that in 300 years of Charleston history no house has *ever* sold for $100,000?" I felt like the naive visitor who came to New York and bought the Brooklyn Bridge.

The Roper House in Charleston was the first real house I had owned, if one excludes the New York co-op. The big Ionic columns that had been built by Robert William Roper, a planter, in 1838 seemed straight out of *Gone With the Wind*, except even grander than Twelve Oaks or Tara. (Years later, Alexandra Ripley, who wrote *Scarlett*, a sequel to *GWTW*, described this house as "Rhett Butler's mother's house in Charleston.") Although Mrs. Hastie, who could have admirably portrayed Mrs. Butler, retained the most handsome floor, I commissioned Tony Hail to create a *pied-à-terre* for me on the third (top) floor, with its magnificent view of the harbor.

Mrs. Hastie lived happily and elegantly for another fourteen years—to age ninety—before I gained possession of the entire house. But I never minded; the top floor *pied-à-terre* was all I needed on weekend trips to Charleston. Tony Hail filled it with an eclectic mixture of English and oriental furnishings, including the beautiful coromandel screen which later got away.

My enthusiasm for Charleston also led me to become involved, as the lead investor and organizer, in rebuilding an antebellum hotel in downtown historic Charleston. The hotel, known as the Mills House, had been built in 1853, at the high-water mark of pre-Civil War prosperity in Charleston. Tony Hail, drawing on his southern origins, whipped up a mid-nineteenth-century Victorian American setting which seemed perfect for this "new" 237-room hotel—a replica of the original—which we reopened with great fanfare in 1970. There was even something for the modernists in the form of a plantation-inspired but very contemporary dining room designed by John Dickinson, a San Francisco designer who collaborated with Tony on this project. Dickinson, now deceased, still enjoys an *avant garde*, almost cult-like reputation. I think the highly original and stylish dining room he did for the Mills House was his best work, though few of his West Coast fans ever got to see it.

Rebuilding the Mills House Hotel was the first major investment by anyone (other than the U. S. Government) in downtown Charleston in the post-World War II period. (This time I *really* did buy the equivalent of the Brooklyn Bridge!) While we struggled with cost over-runs and low occupancy in the early years, the hotel's subsequent success turned the tide of apathy about the economics of downtown Charleston, which today is a vibrant urban environment, with the restored Mills House still serving as one of the anchors. Some of the 1970 Hail-Dickinson interiors still survive. At the time it opened (or, more

The Greek Revival town house I bought at 27 East 11th Street was distinguished by its high stoop, floor-to-ceiling windows, and wrought-iron grillwork. But my favorite feature was the ancient wisteria, spectacular in bloom, covering the entire front of the house.

aptly, reopened), the Mills House may have been the most elegant small hotel in America.

Meanwhile, back in New York City in early 1969 (following my return from Brussels), I purchased a large Greek Revival town house (circa 1840) at 27 East 11th Street. It seemed a good companion for my classic revival Roper House (1838) in Charleston and

The house at 150 East 38th Street was built on the back of its lot, creating a tranquil courtyard in front.

Edgewater (1820) on the Hudson, which I purchased shortly thereafter. Once again Anthony Hail was summoned to do the interiors. This house, which had wonderful fourteen-foot-high ceilings and tall windows to the floor, had one serious defect—two floors of rent-controlled tenants. Unlike my happy co-existence with Mrs. Hastie in Charleston, the owner/rent-control tenant relationship proved more prickly. The tenant living directly above my bedroom, a dancer in *Hello Dolly*, liked to continue dancing

to loud music after he got home from the theater. My efforts with the NYC Rent Control Bureau to gain occupancy of the entire house were to no avail, and I eventually decided to sell 27 East 11th Street after learning of a charming town house for sale at 150 East 38th Street, which had been the long-time residence of the publisher Cass Canfield.

The "Cass Canfield House," as I called it, also had been built in the 1840s, but had been extensively remodeled, virtually obscuring its origins. It was a smaller house than 27 East 11th Street and somehow had survived despite (or because of) its rather incongruous location—square in the middle of a city block rather than facing directly on the street, as is the case with most New York town houses. The former owner had turned this problem into an opportunity by constructing a charming Regency-style loggia, supported by small columns and wrought-iron grillwork, facing East 38th Street. The back wall of the loggia was pierced on either side by a pair of arched doorways leading seductively into an inner courtyard-garden directly in front of the main house, built on the back end of the lot. Because of this peculiar location, the house not only enjoyed a front garden-courtyard but also had views to the rear gardens of the houses on either side.

The house itself was three stories tall, though the ceiling heights were no more than ten feet, unusually low for a pre-Civil War house when ceilings typically were twelve to fourteen feet high. The first floor had double parlors, typical of the period, with the back parlor in this case used as a dining room. A garden room, for breakfast or whatever, opened off the dining room. There were two decent-sized rooms on each floor, and each room had a fireplace. Especially

Anthony Hail created this Louis XVI-style salon for me at 150 East 38th Street.

agreeable was a large room across the entire front of the second floor, which I used as a library and an office. It looked directly over the garden-courtyard, with its fountain providing a soothing retreat from the traffic on the other side of the outer loggia.

The only word to describe 150 East 38th Street was "cute." Since the rooms were small, it was a bit like a charming dollhouse set down in the middle of Manhattan. Tony Hail was again the decorator, creating a sort of French salon effect with Louis XVI furnishings for the most part.

I probably should never have sold this house since it was unique, the perfect *pied-à-terre* in busy Manhattan, convenient to uptown and downtown

where I worked. But it was not to be. One architectural "last hurrah" awaited me before the onset of tight financial times in the mid-1970s temporarily stopped my "house-aholic" ways. The last trip to the bar for me was my purchase of the great house at One Sutton Place North, which I had walked by and eyed longingly many times when I lived at 455 East 57th Street. When I learned it might be for sale I could not resist at least making a pass at what was arguably the finest town house in Manhattan.

CHAPTER 5

ONE SUTTON PLACE NORTH: THE CROWN JEWEL THAT GOT AWAY

The architectural crown jewel that I bought but then let slip away was One Sutton Place North, which I bought in 1972 and sold a couple of years later. Even the name sounds ritzy—"One Sutton Place North." This neo-Georgian brick house was built on a corner lot in the 1920s by Mrs. William K. Vanderbilt, side-by-side with another, even larger, Georgian mate at Nos. 3-5 Sutton Place North—built double-width on two city lots by Ann Morgan, daughter of financier J.P. Morgan. Mott Schmidt, a fashionable designer of classical homes to New York society at the time, was the architect of both houses. The floor levels of the Vanderbilt and Morgan houses are the same and the exterior architectural fenestration is very similar—giving the impression of one massive brick Georgian town house at the corner of Sutton Place and East 57th Street.

Number One Sutton Place North itself is not all that big—it just *looks* big. The house is only one room (twenty feet) wide, but stretches impressively some seventy feet in length (four stories in height, not counting a full

The blue front door seems to be the only relic of my days at One Sutton Place North.

Mrs. Vanderbilt's house and Ann Morgan's next door anchor a square of elegant town houses (called Sutton Square) which enclose a common garden, built out over East River Drive.

basement floor) all the way to the end of Sutton Place, which terminates in a small park overlooking the East River. The restrained but elegant Georgian entrance doorway is situated in the middle of the long side of the house.

Mrs. Vanderbilt's house and Ann Morgan's next door anchor a square of elegant town houses (called Sutton Square) which enclose a common garden, built out *over* East River Drive, giving a panoramic view of the beauties of the East River. Other houses on the square originally belonged to Elizabeth Arden, Elsie DeWolfe, and Elisabeth Marbury—all formidable society figures in the 1920s. This was clearly a highly successful urban renewal project by women who turned a decrepit neighborhood into Sutton Place, one of the two most fashionable addresses in Manhattan, along with nearby Beekman Place.

Like many great houses, One Sutton Place North has been owned by only a few individuals over the years. After Mrs. Vanderbilt came the legendary Charles Merrill, founder of Merrill Lynch. In buying One Sutton Place, I had hoped some of Merrill's success might rub off on DLJ. The only other owner was Arthur Houghton, who sold One Sutton Place North to me in 1972. Houghton actually lived next door in the house Ann Morgan built (No. 3-5). At the time he had rented One Sutton Place North to the Dutch ambassador to the United Nations.

Somewhere in local cocktail gossip, I heard a rumor that Arthur Houghton planned to give No. 3-5 Sutton Square to the United Nations as a permanent home for the secretary general (he subsequently did). It was also rumored that Houghton first wanted to sell the corner house—One Sutton Place North—which would, of course, help establish the value of his tax deduction on the gift of his adjoining property. I knew both houses well from my days living at 455 East 57th Street, less than half a block away. I had particularly admired One Sutton Place North, which looked like the all-time dream place to live in New York. When I heard it might be for sale, I knew it would be a stretch for me to buy such a house, but I decided to try. I also had a buyer in mind for the house I was then living in at 150 East 38th Street.

I don't believe either of Arthur Houghton's Sutton Square town houses had been listed when I approached him quietly, without the inconvenience of a realtor showing the house. I also was willing to wait for the Dutch ambassador to complete his lease. To make a long story short, Houghton did want to sell and after a series of protracted discussions in his elegant library next door, I bought One Sutton Place

Georgina Fairholme and Harrison Cultra produced an elegant blue-striated drawing room with white silk hangings at the triple windows overlooking the garden and river at One Sutton Place.

North for $450,000, which seemed like a huge sum to me at the time.

When I tell you that One Sutton Place North now has an estimated value of $12-15 million, you will know what a great buy I got that autumn afternoon of 1972 when I shook hands with Arthur Houghton on this deal. But I let it get away from me two years later—probably the worst sale I ever made, even though I doubled my money in selling it.

By the time the Dutch ambassador moved out, another year had passed and so I lived in One Sutton Place North only a little over a year—principally 1974. I had done so many rapid-fire decorating projects with Tony Hail that I decided to call in New York decorators Georgina Fairholme and Harrison Cultra for a quick fix on this grand English-style Georgian house, which basically was in good shape structurally. Georgina had worked with John Fowler at London's prestigious Colefax and Fowler design firm. I felt that she and Harrison, a neighbor in the Hudson Valley, would deliver me a house straight out of the British National Trust, since John Fowler had supervised the decoration of so many Trust properties. In this respect I was not disappointed. They produced an elegant blue-striated drawing room, with handsome white silk hangings at the windows, including the triple window at the end of the drawing room overlooking the garden and East River. The first floor dining room, also opening onto the garden and river, was painted a cheerful pumpkin

The first floor dining room of One Sutton Place North, painted a cheerful pumpkin color, opened directly to the garden.

orange, contrasting with an existing black and white marble floor from Mrs. Vanderbilt's regime. The decorators also produced a comfortable white and green bedroom for me on the third floor, again overlooking garden and river.

Despite the charms of the house and its perfect Manhattan location, I never really got to enjoy it. About the time I moved in, hard times (I mean *big time!*) moved into Wall Street, where I had just become the chief executive officer of Donaldson, Lufkin & Jenrette following the departure of Bill Donaldson, who had been appointed Henry Kissinger's undersecretary of state.

It seemed that everything went wrong that could go wrong (for *everyone*, not just DLJ) on Wall Street in 1974. The year is still painful for me to recount. In brief, the Arab oil embargo and a huge jump in oil prices in 1974 drove interest rates sky high—15% or more—as the Federal Reserve sought to restrain inflation. The stock market collapsed to 577 on the Dow Jones Industrial Average (down 45% from the previous peak just above 1000), and the Securities & Exchange Commission forced the New York Stock Exchange to end its system of fixed commission rates (Why they picked such a chaotic time to unfix rates, which further destabilized things, is beyond me.). Instead of earning the old fixed commission rate of forty cents a share on each share we bought or sold for clients, the average commission rate received by DLJ (and other institutional firms like Goldman Sachs and Morgan Stanley) fell to ten cents a share—equivalent to a 75% price cut in the principal service we were selling. Moreover, turnover—or trading activity—on the Exchange was nearly cut in half as investors sat on their hands and watched in

disbelief as the markets collapsed. Mr. Merrill's house did not exactly seem to be bringing me good luck!

How I and DLJ and others on Wall Street survived that wretched year still puzzles me, but somehow we did. One Sutton Place actually may have been my salvation, though it felt more like an albatross around my neck at the time.

All this gloom and doom was not calculated to make me enjoy my move into the grandeur of One Sutton Place just as my world on Wall Street was collapsing. I also owned two other big houses—Edgewater, on the Hudson, and Roper House, in Charleston. On top of this, I still felt responsible for the Mills House Hotel in Charleston. The Arab oil embargo at the time seemed likely to be the kiss of death for tourism, and we were already struggling to make payments on the hotel's $4 million mortgage (which seemed huge at the time).

With DLJ losing money, threatening even my tiny salary, and my equity in the company apparently of little market value in those depressed times, I calculated that I had other liquid assets of no more than $100,000 versus those massive liabilities and potential liabilities. I was "house poor"—not "land poor," the term we used to use to describe impoverished southern families who owned a lot of land but had no money in the bank.

At one of the darkest moments that year, I remember standing on the street corner across from One Sutton Place, talking to my neighbor, Gustave Levy, the legendary managing partner of Goldman Sachs who owned a co-op apartment across the street from me. In the gloom of the moment, Gus observed, "Dick, you can't afford that house. I couldn't afford where I live if I hadn't bought it at the bottom of the Depression." I replied lamely, "You're probably right." But I also remembered

My third floor bedroom at One Sutton Place North, featuring favorite architectural drawings by Harold Sterner, overlooked the East River.

words of advice I had received from another legendary European financier, Baron Edmond Rothschild, who had attended a cocktail party at my house earlier in the year. Edmond loved the house, and as we stood together looking out over the garden and river he remarked, "Dick, you must never sell this house!"

Both were right. From a long-term point of view, I should never have sold the house. One Sutton Place North was "one of a kind," and when you have something unique you should never sell. But Gus Levy was also right. I knew I was badly overextended, yet remembering Baron Rothschild's words I could never bring myself to call a realtor and put the house on the

market. I also knew it would be the wrong time to sell, given the disastrous conditions on Wall Street. New York City real estate always seems to move in synch with the stock market.

What seemed like divine deliverance from my conundrum came a few months or so later in the form of a telephone call from Mrs. H.J. Heinz. Apparently out of the blue (unless Gus Levy put her up to it, which I doubt), Mrs. Heinz—whom I had not known before — called and said, "Oh Mr. Jenrette, is there any way you would ever consider selling your house? I've always wanted to own it." She added that she had bid on it years ago when it was auctioned out of the Merrill estate but had not bid high enough. The fact that Mrs. Heinz had come to me, unsolicited as far as I was concerned, greatly strengthened my hand. Had I put the house up for sale through a realtor, at that particularly distressed time, it would have looked like an act of desperation. So I replied as coolly as possible, "No, it's not for sale, but I've always said if someone offered me one million dollars, I would at least consider the offer." She airily replied, "Oh, that's no problem." Next thing I knew, I was selling One Sutton Place to her.

I actually ended up with something just under $1 million, but this was still double the $450,000 price I had paid for the house two years earlier—half of which I had borrowed. So the return on investment was

startlingly good, especially since everything else in the world seemed to have gone way down in value in 1974. With the sale to Drue Heinz, who still owns the house, I was able to put my financial house in order, get completely out of debt, and still have ample liquid reserves.

This sale, while seemingly disastrous versus today's $12-15 million estimated value for One Sutton Place North, nevertheless gave me peace of mind and the confidence to carry on the fight to save DLJ, which was experiencing its darkest days. After I first moved into Charles Merrill's old house, it seemed the house was bringing me anything but the good luck I had hoped. But in the end the house did bring me good luck, and this windfall gain from the sale gave me the financial leeway to ride out the storm on Wall Street while hanging on to my other "crown jewels"— Edgewater and the Roper House, and, above all, my then badly depressed DLJ stock. I also consoled myself that I was leaving One Sutton Place in good hands; I knew Mrs. Heinz had the financial resources and desire to properly maintain and improve the house.

My saddest moment came on the final night I spent there (before moving into a spartan two-room apartment on 54th Street). I remember walking down the grand spiral staircase and thinking, "This is the first time in my life I have ever gone backward." I wondered if I had peaked in my life at age forty-five. There was no way of knowing that the best was yet to be.

On my final night at One Sutton Place, I remember walking down the grand staircase and thinking, "This is the first time in my life I have ever gone backward." I kept the English Regency mirror and hall chandelier, both now at 67 East 93rd Street.

CHAPTER 6

MY CONVERSION
TO AMERICANA

While my Days of Empire and buying old houses came to a screeching halt as we struggled to keep DLJ alive in the difficult 1970s, I was not so poor, after the sale of One Sutton Place, that I couldn't eke out funds for an occasional piece of antique furniture, if it seemed extraordinary and the price was right. With the two big classical revival houses that I still retained, there was plenty of space to fill up and things that needed upgrading. Poking around antique shops provided some form of relief for me (like Nero fiddling while Rome burned?) from the perils of Wall Street. Also there were some *fabulous* bargains available at that difficult time (mid-'70s). The modernist movement, although getting a little shaky itself, had made antique furniture unfashionable (especially American antiques; in the Vietnam-anguished '70s there seemed to be a loss of pride in the U.S.). The weak economy and depressed stock market also meant that there were few buyers and

"Why don't you try one American piece of that same period? You will find the scale is just right for the house. If you do, I predict over time the American furniture will drive out the English."

– Fred J. Johnston

Among the original furnishings now back at Edgewater is this portrait of Mrs. Robert Donaldson, by George Cook, her harp, and a bust of her father Judge William Gaston, by Ball Hughes.

many sellers. I was able to pick up some extraordinary pieces at what turned out to be bargain prices by continuing to search the field for beautiful furniture and *objets d'art*.

The closest antique shop in the vicinity of my weekend home—Edgewater, my ultimate refuge from the cares of business—was Fred J. Johnston's shop, just across the Hudson River in Kingston, New York. Fred specialized only in American-made furniture, with a concentration on New York furniture of the Federal period (1800-1820) and late-eighteenth-century American, which looked more English to me. Johnston, who told me he had been an advisor to Henry F. du Pont in selecting furniture for his Winterthur Museum, mixed antiques and amusing anecdotes about the great collectors he had known, including du Pont, who apparently had been instrumental in helping Fred set up his own antique business. Fred J. Johnston Antiques became a favorite haunt of mine for weekend browsing, although I had never bought American antiques previously.

Fred remarked to me one day, perhaps in frustration after I had looked and looked on many visits while never buying, "Dick, you have two of the greatest American houses (he was referring to Edgewater and Roper House)

The small lyre-form card table was the first American antique I bought. The portrait of Julia Livingston by John Vanderlyn and the Duncan Phyfe side chairs all belonged to the Livingston family.

of the early nineteenth century, yet you have all English furniture in them. Why don't you *try* one American piece of that same period? You will find the scale is just right for the house. If you do, I predict over time the American furniture will drive out the English."

Fred's money-back offer if I didn't like the piece, plus his Oracle of Delphi-like prediction, were sufficient to induce me to buy a small New York mahogany card table, circa 1820, with a lyre-form base. I had to admit that it looked perfect once installed in the front hall at

Edgewater (twenty-five years later it's still there). Johnston's prediction that the American furniture would eventually drive out the English furnishings also proved correct. Over the years, I sold or gave away (to museums, etc.) most of my English antiques.

Fred Johnston does not deserve all the credit (or blame, if you think like my mother did—that all this collecting of old things was madness) for my conversion to American-made furniture of the early nineteenth century. Dick Button, one of America's all time great Olympic Gold Medal ice skating champions and a friend of many years, also encouraged me to start buying American antiques for my houses. Dick already had a sizable start on his own superb collection of New York Federal and Empire furniture. Through Dick I was introduced to Berry Tracy, curator of the American Wing at the Metropolitan Museum of Art and a great aficionado of New York Federal furniture of the 1800-1820 period. Berry had started Dick on his collection. But the greatest influence on me by far during my apprentice period as a collector of American antiques and old houses was Edward Vason Jones.

Ed Jones, whose name sounds ordinary, was an extraordinary person who became sort of a father figure to me as I launched into collecting Americana in a major way. A dignified and reserved native of Albany, Georgia, Mr. Jones (as most people formally addressed him) was an architect of the old school by training, having done apprentice work with some of Atlanta's great classical architects of the 1920s—Hal Hentz, Neel Reid, and especially Philip Shutze—when Coca-Cola money built some of America's finest suburban homes in Atlanta. Jones and his wife, Maria, also had lived in Savannah, Georgia during World War II, renting an apartment in that city's fabled circa 1820 Owens-Thomas House, the grandest example of Regency architecture in the grand city of Savannah. This house, designed by British architect William Jay, left its mark forever on Ed and Maria Jones (Maria became an equal enthusiast of Federal and Empire furnishings and classical American architecture).

Mr. Jones managed to work his way up the ladder of classical architects (in truth there were not many left in the 1970s), becoming the official architect of the White House under three presidents—Richard Nixon, Gerald Ford and Jones' fellow Georgian, Jimmy Carter. Jones had also done the interior furnishings of the governor's mansion in Georgia, so the Carters must have felt at home in the White House with its Ed Jones-designed Federal-period interiors. For the record, Mr. Jones always credited Pat Nixon (not Jacqueline Kennedy) as being the principal driving force in creating an authentic American ambiance at the White House. Having heard all sides, I still give Jackie seminal credit for returning elegance to the White House, never mind the fact that her principal advisor, Janssen, was French. She was only following in the footsteps of Jefferson, Madison and Monroe, all Francophiles. Mrs. Nixon, however, under Ed Jones' tutelage, made more of an effort to return the original American Federal-period furnishings to the White House.

Ed Jones also was principal advisor and architect-designer to Clement Conger in his monumental task of creating the U.S. State Department's elegant Diplomatic Reception Rooms, which Jones fashioned out of a vast modernist wasteland in the post-World War II State Department building. Jones' unique contribution lay in his knowledge of both American classical architecture

A "porthole" portrait of George Washington by Rembrandt Peale and a rare French clock by DuBuc with Washington's statue, set a patriotic tone in one of the double parlors at Roper House.

and furnishings. The Jefferson Room, which he created in the State Department, is perhaps the consummation of Ed Jones' best work. *The New York Times* called it the finest Palladian room in America. Jones had no peer in his field during his reigning years from the late 1960s to 1980, when he passed away in his early seventies—a great loss to the classical American renaissance that he helped start. He was a great mentor to me.

Ed Jones was backed up by David Richmond Byers, a talented Atlanta decorator who often assisted Ed, and

*This handsome portrait of Robert Donaldson, by
C.R. Leslie, found its way back to Edgewater from Spain!
He now presides over an ensemble of Livingston family
furnishings, including a monogrammed set of French
porcelain placed on a Federal-period sideboard.*

the able firm of Browne & Company, an old-line
decorating firm in Atlanta (sadly, no longer in business)
that made the most elegant draperies I've ever seen,
including most of the present hangings at the White
House and the State Department. Scarlett O'Hara
would have had no trouble making a ball gown had she
ripped down some of Browne & Company's beautiful
draperies! Jones' right-hand man in all his construction
projects was the master craftsman, Odolph Blaylock.

For architectural woodwork and details, Jones had
the highly skilled carver, Herbert Millard, and for
plasterwork, including authentic classic center
medallions for chandeliers, David Flaherty. Together
these talented individuals made an incredible team
under Edward Jones' direction—the renaissance of the
spirit of Jefferson, Madison and Monroe.

While I have noted the absence of books on the
design careers of Otto Zenke and Anthony Hail, there
is an excellent book available on the work of Edward
Vason Jones [*Edward Vason Jones, Architect,
Connoisseur, and Collector* by William R. Mitchell, Jr.,
1995, distributed by the University of Georgia Press.].

Like Otto Zenke had done for me with English
architecture, Ed Jones helped focus my mind on the
fine nuances of American classical architecture as well
as his favorite New York Federal-period furnishings.
I first met Ed at a National Trust for Historic Preservation
meeting in Charleston in 1970, the year we completed
the Mills House Hotel. Jones had heard of my houses,
especially the Roper House in Charleston and
Edgewater on the Hudson. I, in turn, was impressed not
only by his credentials as White House architect, but
the excellent advice on architecture and collecting he
so willingly dispensed to all converts who would listen.
This was a period when the last of the *ancien régime* of
American classical architects would tutor anyone who
would acknowledge there was more to architecture than
Bauhaus modernism. This was before author Tom Wolfe
drove a stake in the heart of "modern" architecture with
his deliciously cutting book, *From Bauhaus to Our House.*

Aided and abetted by Ed Jones, Fred Johnston,
Dick Button, Berry Tracy and others (loosely referred
to as the "Empire Mafia"), I began the process of

converting my collections at Edgewater and Roper House to American Empire furnishings. Their advice to me was to *concentrate my collection*—not just to American furniture but specifically to New York-made furniture, which was the finest available in America in the early nineteenth century. With the opening of the Erie Canal in 1820, New York quickly outstripped Philadelphia, Boston and Charleston as the richest, most sophisticated market. Duncan Phyfe towered above other New York furniture makers of the period, although the much smaller quantity of Charles Honoré Lannuier furnishings may exceed Phyfe in elegance. In the pursuit of Phyfe and Lannuier furniture, all of us in the "Empire Mafia" were keen competitors with one another despite our friendship. I remember once flipping a coin with Dick Button as to which of us would bid on an Empire mirror at Sotheby's. Normally, we were not that friendly with one another when a great piece of furniture came on the market. Some in the Empire Mafia were downright sneaky when it came to the pursuit of a great treasure.

Aside from the fact that my houses were all built in the early nineteenth century, I was attracted to American furniture of this period because it was unique—an amalgam of English, French and other European tastes—unlike American-made furniture of the eighteenth century which largely copied the English model. The early nineteenth century also witnessed the final flowering of hand-carved furniture, before machine-made furniture took over as we moved into the Industrial Revolution of the mid-nineteenth century. For better or worse, I decided this was the period in which I would concentrate my collection, especially the work of Duncan Phyfe.

By concentrating on that one fairly narrow period—New York-made furniture of 1800-1840—I had a fighting chance to become something of an expert, with knowledge of what was first-class and, importantly, what was a fair price. I began to buy at auctions and out of private collections (especially in Charleston and the Hudson Valley, both of which are great repositories of fine furniture). And, of course, I did some buying at Fred Johnston and the leading American antique dealers in New York (Ginsburg, Levy and Sack—the great names of American dealers—and a more recent arrival, George Subkoff). By concentrating my collection, I became known to the trade as a buyer of that particular period and would receive calls from dealers, the auction houses, or other individuals alerting me to new "treasures" (as Fred Johnston called his antiques) that became available. I no longer had to browse; the market often would come to me.

So despite no new houses in the difficult 1970s, I had a lot of fun collecting and restoring antiques. Many of the things I bought required repairs or restoration, and in each case, I followed Berry Tracy's dictum of "getting things ready for the next 100 years." In recent years some revisionists among the ranks of professional conservators have argued that Ed Jones and Tracy sometimes *over* restored things. Having heard these arguments, I still believe that American Empire furniture, which was embellished originally by showy gilt or ebonized paw feet, ormolu mounts, elaborate stenciling, beautifully polished mahogany, etc. simply does not look attractive if things are left discolored and dark. Jones and Tracy brought back the glitter that restored Federal and Empire furniture to popularity. The best examples of their handiwork are at the White House, the State Department and the Metropolitan Museum. I rest my case.

CHAPTER 7

THE RETURN OF PROSPERITY
(AND MORE OLD HOUSES)

My exile from great Manhattan houses lasted about two years. After selling One Sutton Place North, I purchased a small two-room co-op apartment at 17 East 54th Street. Its amenities included a large living room, a bedroom plus kitchen and bath. It did have one distinctive feature—a wrap-around terrace that overlooked the Museum of Modern Art garden across the street and twenty floors below. My apartment was on the top floor of this once terribly modern art deco building, dating from the 1930s, so the small abode bore the rather grand nomenclature of "Penthouse," or so it was described in the elevator. Aside from the view of MOMA's elegant sculpture garden below, I had a spectacular in-your-face view of the midtown Manhattan skyline, especially appealing at night.

In short, I wasn't really "roughing it," especially since I could escape to Edgewater or Charleston on

Relief came at last in 1978 when I heard about a charming New York City town house, built in 1826, at 37 Charlton Street in lower Manhattan.

weekends. Also, this was such a difficult time on Wall Street (the mid-1970s) that I probably would not have been doing much entertaining even had I hung on to One Sutton Place. My new *pied à terre* was perfect to have one or two friends in for cocktails and a view of the skyline. Also, I was right in the middle of the best restaurant area of Manhattan; everything was in walking distance, except grocery stores. But art deco architecture was never my *shtick*, nor did I like apartment living; going up and down public elevators all the time was boring and time consuming. I never saw this apartment as my permanent abode in Manhattan.

The gloom that pervaded Wall Street and the U. S. economy for most of the 1970s began to lift as we neared the end of the decade, and, with renewed prosperity, my latent interest in old houses began to reassert itself. While I had managed to hang on to my two great houses outside Manhattan, I was never really happy in the two-room *pied-à-terre* in New York City that I had moved into after selling glamorous One Sutton Place North. The comedown from living in one of the grandest town houses in Manhattan—and certainly the best address—to a two-room apartment,

The double parlors at 37 Charlton Street, architecturally unchanged since the house was built in 1826, were decorated in a late Federal-style for me by Edward Vason Jones. Most of the furniture is Phyfe, and the portrait is of Andrew Jackson by Ralph Earl, Jr.

practical though it might have been under the circumstances, was hard on my psyche. Moreover, all those American antiques I had been buying did not *at all* fit into this late 1930s art deco-style apartment on East 54th Street.

Relief came at last in 1978 when I heard about a charming New York City town house, built in 1826, at 37 Charlton Street in lower Manhattan. The house seemed perfect—it had been virtually untouched in its 150-year history, but structurally was still sound. All the original black marble mantels, moldings, doors and windows were intact. Almost miraculously, the house had never been chopped up and subdivided into apartments, a common fate of early New York City town houses.

Edward Jones checked the house out for me and pronounced it a near-perfect specimen of the late Federal/early Greek Revival style so popular in the 1820s. This was a period of great optimism and expansion in New York City, with the opening of the Erie Canal in 1820, linking the Port of New York to shipping from the Great Lakes. The house at No. 37 Charlton Street had been built on speculation by John Jacob Astor as part of a row of town houses. The high ceilings and late Federal-period architectural detail seemed perfect for my burgeoning collection of American antiques.

And, finally, the price was right—$250,000, which seemed cheap at the time for a complete town house, though lower Manhattan was still considered unfashionable. (Nine years later, I sold it for $2 million before moving back uptown.) Since I worked on Wall Street at that time, the downtown location was actually very convenient. And so I happily grabbed it, saying good-bye to apartment living forever, I hoped.

Working with Ed Jones on restoring and decorating this old house at 37 Charlton Street was lots of fun and very educational. Ed, with the help of David Byers and Browne & Company, which made the draperies, created a classic Federal-period setting. Most of the furniture I used in the house had been made in New York by Duncan Phyfe at about the same time the house was constructed. As Fred Johnston had predicted, the scale of this furniture seemed just right for the house. The restored house and its contents gleamed. Burnished gold convex mirrors (Ed Jones *loved* convex mirrors and played a seminal role in returning them to popularity in America.) stood out sharply against the paint colors Ed selected for the walls—dusty yellow, rose, and beige. His favorite line to Jack Smith, who mixed a lot of the paint colors in the house, was "Put a little more umber in that, Jack." We heard that over and over, but Ed Jones' "umbered down colors" really showed off the gold frames and brightly colored Federal-period and Regency colors in the silk fabrics (many of which were stripes) that Mr. Jones favored. It was an interesting contrast to Tony Hail, who preferred "clear" colors. Another favorite technique of Ed Jones was marbleizing walls, especially in entrance halls. His favorite marbleizer was the talented Robert Jackson, who turned out to be a neighbor of mine in the Hudson Valley. Over the years, Jackson marbleized so many walls for me that I began to nickname him "Stonewall" Jackson!

At the same time, Ed Jones was working on his massive project in Washington, D. C. to convert the dismal U.S. State Department reception rooms into an elegant suite of Federal-period rooms. At 37 Charlton Street, I used many of the same artisans who worked for

Ed and Clem Conger in their spectacularly successful conversion of this space into a diplomatic *tour de force*.

I was so pleased with the stunning Federal-period setting that Ed Jones and David Byers did for me at 37 Charlton that I also used them in redecorating the offices of Donaldson, Lufkin & Jenrette, which by the late '70s was returning to prosperity. Even today, after DLJ's move uptown to 277 Park Avenue, the look of the offices is vintage Ed Jones' Federal period. Mark Hampton, who together with DLJ's curator, Margize Howell, coordinated the decorating in DLJ's new offices, kept the Federal-period look that Ed Jones and David Byers had given us, including recycling many of the window curtains, wallpaper and carpets, as well as all the Federal-period antiques in DLJ's collection. "Stonewall" Jackson and his fellow artists must have marbleized a mile of hallways in DLJ's new quarters.

With an appropriate setting at last for my antiques and lifestyle in Manhattan (both at home and work), a choice weekend house on the Hudson, and a stake in the Old South through my Charleston house, I felt I was set with all the material things that one could possibly desire in this life. About that same time, I also sold the Mills House Hotel in Charleston at a reasonable price, thereby removing another contingent liability (When hard times came, I was the bank of last resort for the hotel.). Business was good and I began to relax and savor my collection of fine old houses and antiques.

But as events unfolded, my days of collecting old houses and antiques were far from over. In 1984, ten years after the worst business year of my life, The Equitable Life Assurance Society proposed to buy DLJ for what at the time seemed like a fancy price— $440 million or two times our company's book value,

Only an Aries like me would want a red library. I enjoyed working at 37 Charlton Street at this tall New York secretary and bookcase.

or net asset value. After the ten-year struggle to save the company during the difficult 1970s, I think we were all tired. The price offered was all cash at a big premium to the market price, which made our shareholders very happy. For the first time in my life I had considerable cash in the bank. Predictably, this newfound wealth once again led to more "adventures with old houses."

First came Ayr Mount, the ancestral home of the Kirkland family in Hillsborough, North Carolina (about thirty miles from Raleigh, my birthplace and hometown). I was giving a speech at nearby Chapel Hill when John Sanders, a good friend and fellow architectural buff, said, "Dick, I know you don't want to buy another house, but I think you would enjoy looking at Ayr Mount. It has some extraordinary interior woodwork." Since I had some spare time,

The approach to Ayr Mount, built in 1814, was a straight driveway off the old Halifax Road. No nonsensical curves for the thrifty Scottish builder, William Kirkland.

I accepted John's invitation to visit Ayr Mount and was quite smitten at first sight. I had secretly nurtured visions of retiring and returning home one day to my native North Carolina to teach or go back to school at either Duke University or the University of North Carolina at Chapel Hill. Both were only ten miles from Ayr Mount. Thus, the location and thoughts of retirement provided some justification for my apparent folly in buying yet another old house. I still had many of my closest friends in North Carolina but owned nothing in my home state. Once again the price seemed right ($450,000 for the house and 52 acres of beautiful rolling countryside in the heart of the booming Raleigh-Durham-Chapel Hill Research Triangle).

Ayr Mount, built of brick made on the property, was constructed between 1814-1816. Unlike my other, more pretentious houses, Ayr Mount is far more spartan on the exterior, befitting its thrifty Scottish builder, William Kirkland. The interior woodwork, however, is lavish—a sort of vernacular Georgian interspersed with Gothic touches—very unusual at this time and place. There's nothing quite like it in North Carolina. It has the finest interior woodwork by far in the central Carolina region in which I grew up. Fashions moved slowly in early-nineteenth-century North Carolina, which perhaps explains why Ayr Mount looks more like a late-eighteenth-century house despite its documented early-nineteenth-century completion date.

Prior to my purchase, only members of the Kirkland family—five generations—had owned Ayr Mount. Many of the original furnishings, including a portrait of the first owner, William Kirkland, were still there. I was able to acquire most of these furnishings with the purchase of the house. Edward Jones had passed away shortly before I bought Ayr Mount, but Todd Dickinson, a local contractor, undertook a much needed and extensive restoration of the old house. David Byers and Browne & Company picked up where Ed left off on

decorating the house. A year later, Ayr Mount was beautifully restored and elegantly draped and furnished in the best Federal-period traditions.

Even before work was completed on Ayr Mount, I was bitten again by the old house bug—this time an old sugar cane plantation in St. Croix, in the distant U.S. Virgin Islands. Talk about money burning a hole in my pocket! A year previously I had rented Estate Cane Garden for a week's winter vacation, and had enjoyed the old house with its own beach and unique setting overlooking the Caribbean. I idly remarked to the daughter of the owner that I might be interested if the family ever decided to sell (this was, of course, before I bought Ayr Mount). When the owner died the following year, her daughter called to see if I still wanted to buy Cane Garden. Although I was still busy restoring Ayr Mount my predictable "house-aholic" answer was yes. It seemed the perfect winter retreat, and I still had some idea of imminent retirement after selling DLJ to Equitable. The idea of owning such a house in the Caribbean seemed exotic and totally irresistible.

Cane Garden was an old Danish sugar cane plantation, built in the late eighteenth century and remodeled in my favorite neo-classical style (with the obligatory Doric columns) around 1820. The original house had burned at the turn of the twentieth century, but the house had been rebuilt using the massive two-and-one-half-foot-thick stone walls that had survived. I was drawn to the house principally by its location—on a high hill overlooking the blue Caribbean, with nearly a mile of beachfront. My rationale (I always seemed to feel I needed a "rationale"; it was not enough just to *want* something.) was that the house and grounds would be a great long-term investment with all the beachfront—

and a "fun investment" as well. Since I really didn't need another house, especially in St. Croix—2,000 miles south of my New York home base—I was able to bargain and purchase the property on what seemed to be favorable terms, as was the case with Ayr Mount.

While I may have bought both Ayr Mount and Cane Garden relatively cheaply, what I failed to consider was my own expensive proclivity to take things back to their original state. It took over a year of hard work by Todd Dickinson, my contractor, and $1 million, far more than I had spent before on restoring houses, to get Ayr Mount back to its original pristine state, with the cost of rehabilitation dwarfing my original $450,000 investment in house and grounds. But it is, without doubt, the single most professional restoration job I've undertaken, even down to the discovery of the original colors. And it has worked perfectly since then.

If I was a bit shocked by the high cost of restoring Ayr Mount, worse news lay ahead for me at Cane Garden where I had a naive view that labor and building costs might be cheap in the Virgin Islands. Three years later and $3 million poorer (*double* what I paid for Cane Garden house and grounds) I had completely rebuilt Cane Garden and returned it as nearly as possible to its original state as a Danish "Great House." The rebuilding costs clearly seemed excessive, and I was reminded of the old adage, often quoted by John Castle, one of my former partners at DLJ, "The footprints of the owner are the best manure." I was physically too far from the construction site to monitor what was going on.

Who could resist this small Palladian villa overlooking the blue Caribbean in St. Croix, U.S. Virgin Islands?

While I groused and worried about the time and money I spent on the Cane Garden rebuilding, you will see from the later chapter on this property that I have concluded the final product was worth the effort.

I am almost embarrassed to say that the story of my adventures with old houses didn't end here! After flirting around with the idea of "retiring" to North Carolina or South Carolina to teach or write or drink bourbon, I decided I was too attached to New York City to cut the umbilical cord. Equitable had asked me to become chairman of its board of directors, which sounded like a nice capstone on my career. Given my free-spending ways, it also seemed a good idea to continue working! New York had been my home since leaving Harvard Business School in 1957, and there is something about New York that keeps you young and challenged. So thirty years later, in 1987, I decided to "re-up" (as we used to say in the Army) and stay in New York, abandoning plans for early retirement or a move to academia. I also decided to move back uptown, back to "eastside" Manhattan, which would be more convenient to my work at The Equitable. I wanted a place where I could put down roots for a long time. So I sold my "downtown" brick house at 37 Charlton Street for $2 million—a large gain over my $250,000 cost—and immediately reinvested two times the sale proceeds in a brick town house on East 93rd Street that once had belonged to George F. Baker, the patron saint of Harvard Business School.

Within a week of my purchase of 67 East 93rd Street, which bore a remarkable physical similarity to One Sutton Place North (both houses built in the 1920s), the stock market crashed—down 23% in two horrible days that shook Wall Street in October 1987.

It seemed like Yogi Berra's *"déjà vu* all over again," since something similar had happened not long after I bought One Sutton Place. Remembering what happened in 1929, I wondered if these 1920s houses might be jinxed! But "this too shall pass" proved to be the case once again as the stock market soon recovered, this time much more quickly than in the 1970s.

This alarming drop in the market did turn out to be a harbinger of more difficult economic times, which

Millford Plantation, built in 1840, is quite simply the finest Greek Revival house in the South, perhaps in the nation.

made my sojourn as chairman of The Equitable Life Assurance Society anything but a lark as I passed age sixty. Before it was all over, I had become the company's chief executive officer and led it through an arduous process called "demutualization," converting from a mutual ownership structure in which the company was owned by its policyholders to public ownership. The more than $2 billion of new capital we raised in the process saved The Equitable, and the company has now moved to new heights and I am happily retired.

After the rescue of Equitable from the brink of disaster, I must have subconsciously decided it was time to reward myself—one more old house, and that was Millford Plantation in South Carolina, probably the most extraordinary of all my houses. Once again, I came upon it by accident. I had absolutely no intention of buying another house. Built in 1840 with massive Corinthian fluted columns, Millford almost makes Ashley Wilkes' Twelve Oaks in *Gone With The Wind* look shabby! It also contained large quantities of the original antique furniture—by Duncan Phyfe, no less! And in this case, after my initial infatuation, I discovered the house had even been built by a distant Hampton relative of mine.

What was the rationalization for this final purchase? There was none, other than that this was, quite simply, the finest Greek Revival house in the South, perhaps in the nation. I really wanted to see it restored to its original glory. Following the purchase of Millford, I began to think that one day I might contribute all my historic houses to a foundation that would preserve them for posterity and open them to the public. To this end, I established Classical American Homes Preservation Trust—quite a mouthful, but it describes my houses. And as a gesture to fiscal prudence, I donated Ayr Mount to this new foundation since I rarely used this house following the Millford Plantation purchase. But I could not bear to sell Ayr Mount after all the painstaking restoration efforts. Also, I did not want to cut this tie to my native North Carolina. Ayr Mount

and its valuable collection of Federal furnishings, many of which are original to the house, is now open to the public for tours under the auspices of Preservation North Carolina.

So there you have it—perhaps the all-too-complete description of my odyssey with old houses and antiques. Exhausting? Yes. Fun? Most of the time. Would I do it again? Absolutely. Recommend for others? Unconditionally. Most important to me, I believe I have had a role in creating beauty—at least in restoring these beautiful old houses and antiques to their former glory and preserving them as models for future generations to enjoy. Nothing pleases me more than to share these houses with sympathetic visitors who, hopefully, will be inspired to return to their home communities and follow my example.

Over the last decade, more than 100,000 people have visited my houses on group tours, even though, with the exception of Ayr Mount, none are open to the public. At times I get overwhelmed with tours and tour requests, but I try to accommodate as many as possible. Despite all the minimalist-modernism of much of the post-World War II period, I never cease to be amazed at how many people still love old houses and antiques. There's no place like home—the older the better.

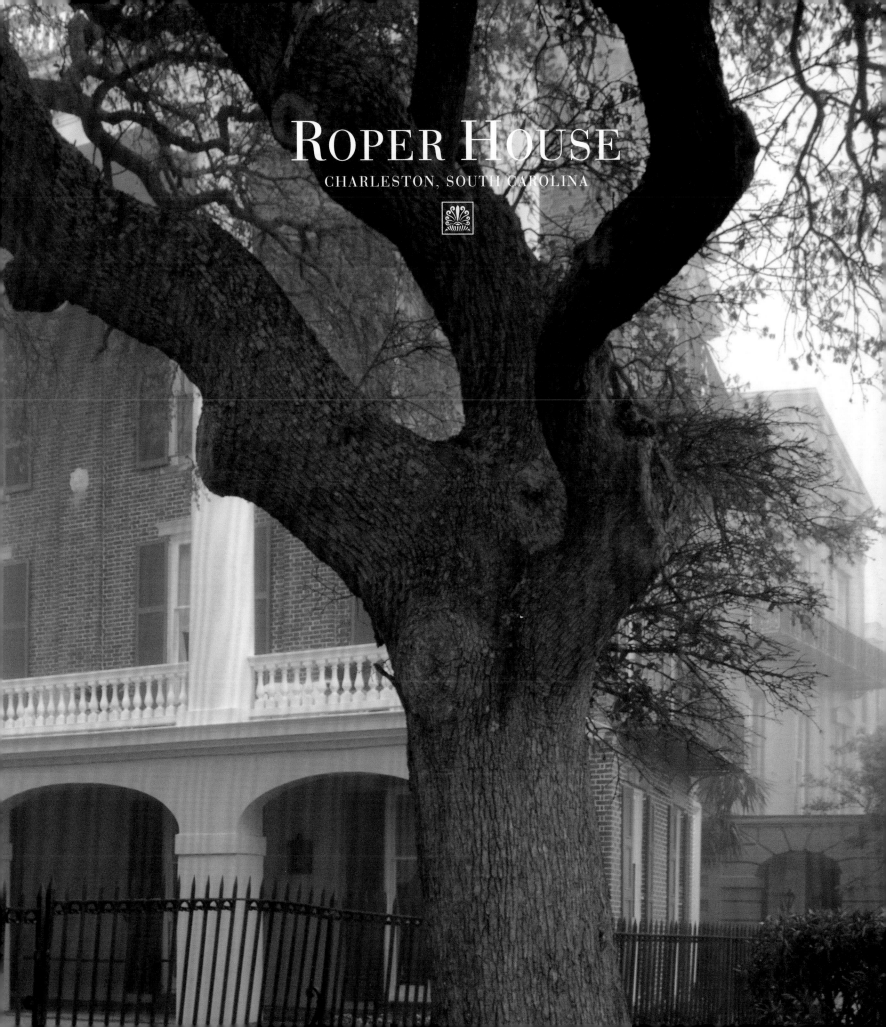

ROPER HOUSE

CHARLESTON, SOUTH CAROLINA

CHAPTER 8

THE ROPER HOUSE:
HOW IT ALL GOT STARTED

The first house I owned outright (excluding my New York City co-op) was the Roper House, a magnificent Greek Revival mansion at 9 East Battery in Charleston, South Carolina. I bought it in 1968, the 130th anniversary of the house's completion in 1838 and just short of my own fortieth birthday. Although I did not realize it at the time, this purchase was the beginning of my hobby of collecting old houses and antiques, which continues unabated more than thirty years later. The fact that I did not begin my acquisitive habits until age forty is evidence that you don't have to be a *wunderkind* to start your own collection.

The Roper House, with its magnificent Ionic columns overlooking the sea, seemed to me the quintessential antebellum mansion that my *Gone With the Wind*-influenced generation dreamed about owning, although Roper House is a town house and not a plantation. Not only is the house stunning architecturally, it has an unsurpassed location at the

Roper House, with its magnificent Ionic columns overlooking the sea, seemed to me the quintessential antebellum mansion that my Gone With the Wind-influenced generation dreamed about owning.

(Preceding and left) The Roper House overlooks Charleston's historic harbor, including Fort Sumter, where the Civil War began.

head of Charleston's High Battery, a gigantic sea wall built in the early nineteenth century to reclaim swampy land and hold back floods and hurricanes. From the great piazza of the Roper House, one looks out directly over Charleston Harbor to Fort Sumter, where the Civil War began, and beyond that to the Atlantic Ocean. There is even a piece of the barrel of the largest Confederate cannon, which blew up in front of the house, embedded in the roof, where it has remained since 1865. And, of course, Charleston itself is one of the prettiest cities in America. For in-city living, you could not find a better location or a more elegant house architecturally—at least that is my boast. I've never found a town house anywhere else—including London, Paris or New York—that matches the Roper House from an all-around point of view.

It is the tradition in Charleston to call houses by their builder's name, so 9 East Battery will never be known as the "Jenrette House." Robert William Roper, the builder, was a planter whose father, Thomas Roper, had built and owned an earlier, less imposing town house still standing a block or so further up East Battery. The Ropers claimed direct descent from

*The piazza of Roper House, with tall Ionic columns framing
a view to the Atlantic Ocean, is everyone's favorite place for
a party, especially when a full moon rises out of the water.*

ROPER HOUSE
Floor Plan

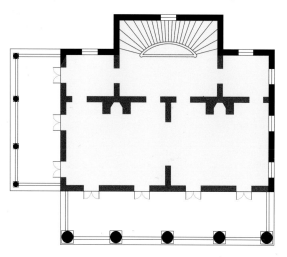

Margaret Roper, a daughter of Sir Thomas More.
The younger Roper, who married Martha Rutledge
Laurens, was a civic leader, elected to the state
legislature and chairman of the important agriculture
committee. He was also quite articulate, judging by
several of his speeches which were published in
pamphlet form. In one celebratory Fourth of July
speech (when that occasion was more popular in the
South before the Civil War), Roper boasts about
America's growing roster of prominent native artists.
His list of American artists, including Trumbull,
Stuart, Peale and Sully, was remarkably prescient,
judging by the number that have stood the test of time
and remain popular today.

The Roper wealth seemed to come from their
plantation—Point Comfort—about fifteen miles up
the Cooper River, which empties into Charleston
Harbor right in front of the Roper House (a site that
Charlestonians, only halfway in jest, describe as
"where the Cooper River and the Ashley River come
together to form the Atlantic Ocean"!).

The architect of Roper House is unknown.
Architectural historians Kenneth and Martha Severens, in
their definitive article on Roper House for *The Magazine
ANTIQUES*, make a persuasive case for Charles Friedrich
Reichardt, a Prussian architect and pupil of Germany's
greatest classical architect Karl Friedrich Schinkel.

*The circular staircase at Roper House ascends through
all three stories, past the Goddess of Literature
(right) and then past the Goddess of Music (center).
Both are original to the house, as is the large red punch
bowl with classical Grecian figures.*

Shown above is my favorite French Empire tall case clock, complete with an ormolu bust of Napoleon, an eagle, and signs of the zodiac surrounding the clock's face. It was found in another old Charleston home and perfectly fits the narrow space between the two doors to the double parlor.

The spectacular double parlors (left and above) of Roper House seem to be made for entertaining. Most of the suite of furniture is by Duncan Phyfe, circa 1815-20. David Byers did the curtains at the windows, which double as doors to the piazza, and Bill Thompson, working with Scalamandré, did the period carpets and silk upholstery. The chandeliers, once gas-lit, were made for the house.

Reichardt arrived in Charleston in 1836, and was the architect of the monumental Charleston Hotel. Both the Charleston Hotel and Roper House bear strong resemblance to Schinkel's much-praised Altes Museum (1822-30) in Berlin, with its long Ionic colonnade and flat roofline, built high above a ground-level arcade. Roper may also have used a local architect, possibly Frederick Wesner, to complete the work, but I believe that Reichardt influenced the bold design of the house. Since Reichardt's work at the Charleston Hotel also was the genesis of the plans for Millford Plantation, he may have been the architect, or at least a consultant, on *both* my South Carolina houses.

The front parlor, overlooking the harbor, seems to be in homage to George Washington. Rembrant Peale's "Porthole Portrait" of Washington hangs above a French Empire mantel clock by DuBuc a Paris, featuring a gilt statue of Washington. A copy of Houdon's bust of Lafayette, Washington's close friend and ally, surveys the ensemble which includes French porcelain of the early nineteenth century.

Like most Charleston houses, Roper House is built with its gable end, or side, directly on the street, with a long piazza to catch sea breezes built along the length of the house, sideways to East Battery. But the similarity to other Charleston houses largely stops there. Charleston's heyday as one of America's four largest and richest cities was in the late eighteenth century, and many of the great houses in this neighborhood were built prior to or just after 1800 in a more restrained "Adam style," a Charleston version of Britain's Adam brothers' architectural style. In contrast, Roper House was built in the much more exuberant Greek Revival style some forty years later when Charleston was seeking to make an economic comeback after steadily losing ground to its northern port rivals—New York, Boston, Philadelphia and Baltimore. The two-story Ionic columns of the Roper House, built on top of an arched loggia across the side of the ground floor, are much larger than the more delicate columns found on most earlier Charleston residences. The effect is far more robust, almost boastful.

Indeed, Robert William Roper had wanted his house to be the first and most prominent to be seen as visitors approached Charleston by sea (ships still were the most important means of travel in the early nineteenth century). At the time the High Battery was completed, the Roper mansion was the first house to be built, standing alone in a large corner plot which is now shared with three other large antebellum mansions—the DeSaussure House, now on the corner, and two Ravenel houses on either side of Roper House. The financial panic of 1837 might have induced Roper to sell some of his choice land. Another local explanation is that Roper's father gave away much of the family fortune to found Roper Hospital (a vibrant Charleston institution today), forcing the son to economize on his dream house. Yet the scale and magnificence of the giant Ionic columns that Roper

Outside the double parlors of the piano nobile, *the stairway continues to the third floor, bypassing another of the Grecian goddesses who guard the way. Curtains by David Byers, painted* trompe l'oeil *floor by Robert Jackson.*

built give the house precedence over its neighbors. Roper House still evokes a gasp of surprise at its massive scale from visitors who pass by today.

When I bought Roper House from Drayton Hastie in 1968 I agreed to a life tenancy for his mother, Sarah Hastie, then in her late seventies and said to be in poor health. Under the agreement Mrs. Hastie would have use of the *piano nobile*—the principal, or second floor of the mansion (with eighteen-foot-high ceilings!)— for the rest of her life. At this time there were two

rental units on the ground floor (in what had been the dining room and library) and a full floor-through apartment on the third, or bedroom floor, which I could use for myself as a *pied-à-terre* in Charleston.

Since I didn't need such a large house in Charleston, and was fully occupied with my work in New York, this arrangement worked exceedingly well, although Mrs. Hastie lived to be ninety—a long time for a life tenancy. When I came to Charleston on weekends, the handsome top floor apartment that Tony Hail decorated for me was certainly adequate for my needs. The deck we put on the roof still has the best view in Charleston.

I also became very fond of Mrs. Hastie, whose elegant lifestyle epitomized the best of Charleston living. I recall being impressed that she slipped into a long velvet evening gown *every* evening before dinner, whether or not she had guests. Miriam, her maid, would offer up the ritual evening bourbon, and Mrs. Hastie would hold court. Being right in the city in such handsome quarters, she never lacked for visitors. I recall her advising me to give my parties there at full moon, which rises in a giant orange ball out of the sea right in front of Roper House, shimmering on the water. Of all my houses and other places visited, I can recall no better place to experience the rising of the full moon.

Mrs. Hastie thoroughly enjoyed her final years to age ninety at Roper House. She kept right on top of current events, had a parade of amusing callers, and the staff to

The first floor reception room might have served as an office for Mr. Roper. The sliding double doors (right) lead to the dining room.

handle them. I recall thinking that this was the perfect retirement home—mild climate, an attractive city, attractive neighbors and interesting out-of-town visitors to Charleston, the availability of help, and excellent medical facilities at the Medical University of South Carolina as well as the house's namesake Roper Hospital.

After Mrs. Hastie passed away, I spent about two years updating and modernizing Roper House, anticipating that I would make greater personal use of it. But it was not to be—yet. My own mother, having turned ninety about the time work was complete on the house, was no longer able to live alone in her house in Florida. Unable to get help for her there and unwilling to put her in a nursing home, my sister, brother and I concluded that the best solution would be to move Mother to Roper House, taking over part of the top floor that I had kept as an apartment. An added inducement was the presence in Charleston of my nephew, Dr. Joseph M. Jenrette III, at the Medical University. This insured the best medical facilities.

The arrangement seemed to work well, and Mother lived to be 101 before she passed away quietly one night. At her advanced age, and not being a Charleston native, she was never able to enjoy the Roper House as Mrs. Hastie had done before her. But the presence of four loyal nurse's aides, operating on three shifts, made life comfortable for her.

Because of my full-time business involvement in New York and the other "second houses" I later bought, I was never bothered by not having full access to Roper House either during Mrs. Hastie's long life tenancy or Mother's subsequent passing the century mark in age there. But I did begin to think I also would have to live to be ninety to get to enjoy the place fully.

While Mother lived on the top floor, I did proceed with my plans to renovate and redecorate the first two floors, including Mrs. Hastie's beloved *piano nobile* with its double parlors and eighteen-foot-high ceilings. David Byers and Browne & Company, who had done all the curtains at the White House and the State Department, created stunning deep blue and gold window draperies for the giant floor-to-ceiling windows, which looked out to sea. Bill Thompson designed, and Scalamandré produced, new wall-to-wall carpets (which came into vogue about the time Roper House was built) also in blue and gold, with classical motifs matching the architecture. The walls throughout the house were marbleized by Robert Jackson, a technique which was rapidly becoming a hallmark of my houses.

The double parlors of the *piano nobile*, each outfitted with original black marble mantels, are filled with a suite of Duncan Phyfe Federal-period furniture with blue silk upholstery. Most of these pieces date from 1800 to 1820, earlier than the house, and probably are a bit overpowered by the huge scale of this Greek Revival suite of rooms. While I keep thinking that the furniture might look better in a Federal-period house, I don't need any more houses (famous last words!). In any event, these Phyfe pieces still manage to look terrific, set off by the elegant window hangings, a Rembrandt Peale porthole portrait of George Washington over one mantel, a Ralph Earl portrait of Andrew Jackson over the other

Floor-length windows in the dining room lead to a garden terrace, my favorite place for breakfast alfresco.

The most comfortable room in Roper House is this third floor living room, for reading, television viewing, or desk work.

The four-poster bed in the master bedroom is positioned to look straight ahead to the Atlantic Ocean. The Ionic capitals of the columns on the piazza are visible out the side windows.

mantel, plus other lesser-known portraits and prints. Atop the front parlor mantel is a rare French-made clock by DuBuc featuring a miniature statue of George Washington, inscribed "First in War, First in Peace, First in the Hearts of his Countrymen." I have three of these George Washington clocks scattered about my houses, while DLJ has a fourth. There's also one in the White House and one at Winterthur. Perhaps we've

cornered the market. The last one to come on the market went for almost $150,000 at auction versus my average cost of $10,000.

The ground floor of Roper House, also with high ceilings, is entered through a long hallway running the length of the house along the north side. There is a sweeping spiral staircase, ascending three floors, on the exterior side of this entrance hall. On the other side, two tall doors lead into a reception room in front and dining room on the rear, divided by double doors. The rooms can be thrown together *en suite* for large dinner parties. Both rooms are decorated in predominantly green and gold colors, with the green carpets seeming to flow right onto the lawn and garden just outside the floor-length windows. Behind the dining room is an outdoor patio overlooking the garden. This is my favorite place for breakfast when I come to Charleston.

The third, or top, floor is now returned to bedroom status, since I changed my living room in front from *pied-à-terre* days back into a luxurious master bedroom. From a big four-poster bed, one looks directly to the Atlantic Ocean through tall windows that extend to the floor, with the original ornamental wrought-iron balconies framing the view. The sky blue curtains and carpet, which seem to merge with the blue-gray ocean outside, have given this bedroom the nickname "Blue Heaven." Also on the third floor, the second of two original bedroom suites has been turned into a library/television/reading room/lounge with comfortable, upholstered furniture (Duncan Phyfe not admitted here). On rainy, cold days in winter this room with a big fireplace, red draperies, and plenty of books is the place to be.

All the rooms that I have described are in the original central block of Roper House, consisting of double parlors on each of the first two floors and a pair of large bedrooms on the third floor—all connected by the majestic circular staircase and hall. But there are many more rooms in a large rear wing, which was not added until 1886 following a disastrous earthquake which badly damaged most of Charleston. The "new wing," now over a hundred years old, was built by the Rudolph Siegling family in a vote of confidence for Charleston's future. It is built on top of what was the original, detached kitchen of Roper House. The new wing contained a kitchen and servants quarters on the first floor, a sixty-foot-long, high-ceilinged ballroom on the second, and two more bedrooms on the third floor. Later, during the Depression of the 1930s, Roper House was sold by the Sieglings to Solomon Guggenheim, who converted the second floor ballroom wing into three more bedrooms. The wealthy Guggenheim, who used the house as a base for hunting and fishing in the South, was a good custodian of the house during the Depression years, when other Charleston houses deteriorated badly. Guggenheim, a mining magnate, was considered one of the nation's richest men at the time (he even built a huge iron vault on the first floor, evidently not fully trusting banks that were failing in the 1930s).

In its now 160 years of existence, Roper House has had only a handful of owners, always a good sign that the house is a nice place to live. Robert William Roper died in 1845 from malaria, and his widow, without children, sold the house in 1851 to the Ravenels, who lived next door. The house was uninhabitable during much of the Civil War because its harborside location was vulnerable to bombardment. The Sieglings bought the house in 1874 and owned it for the next fifty-six years, adding the ballroom wing and repairing the earthquake's damage in 1886. The Guggenheims kept up the house during the ravages of the Great Depression and World War II shortages. The Hasties maintained and loved the house during the post-World War II years before selling it to me in 1968. My thirty-one years of ownership are exceeded in duration only by the Sieglings.

Unlike the situation at my other houses, remarkably few of the original Roper furnishings have found their way back home. This may be my fault for not being more aggressive in pursuing some leads or perhaps I got distracted by buying so many other houses. In comparison with my experiences at the other houses, there are few traces of the Ropers at 9 East Battery, outside of the magnificent house itself. Mrs. Roper's portrait returned briefly after I rescued it from an attic and had the painting restored. But she was reclaimed several years later by a family member. I'm sure there's more Roper memorabilia out there somewhere!

Of all my houses, Roper House really looks and feels like a "party house" (hopefully not of the *Animal House* variety, although it looks suspiciously like a fraternity house with those big columns). Even though I've only given a few large parties here, it works extremely well with crowds. By far the biggest party I have given here was occasioned by the grand opening of the rebuilt Mills House Hotel, in which I (unhappily, for a while) was the lead investor. Some 400 guests, mostly Charlestonians and South Carolinians, but also many friends from North Carolina and New York, filled the lawn, all three floors and the roof. The house didn't even seem crowded. I noted that the most

powerful politicians—Senators Thurmond and Hollings, four governors past and present, and the mayor—all found their way to the power point summit on the roof deck that moonlit evening. But what amazed me was how well traffic flowed within the house with such a large gathering. There were no bottlenecks; each room has several ways of entering and exiting. The high ceilings on the principal floor swallow the noise and give a sense of grandeur, heightened by the house's original crystal chandeliers, which were once gaslit. People seem to love to congregate on the big piazza opening off the double parlors on the second floor. At such times, the house seems alive and fulfilling its destiny.

Having one of the finest houses in town also seems to ensure that I am a stopping-off point for notables visiting Charleston, including Presidents Ford and Bush with their first ladies, The Emperor and Empress of Japan, HRH The Prince of Wales, Lady Thatcher, General Colin Powell, Bishop Tutu from South Africa and assorted Rockefellers and Rothschilds. The house, with its tall Ionic columns invoking memories of Charleston's antebellum wealth, and the spectacular view out to sea never fail to impress.

Prince Charles' stay at Roper House, which lasted several days while he was in Charleston for a conference, was particularly memorable since he arrived only a few weeks after Hurricane Hugo, which had devastated Charleston (including my garden, which was literally swept away). Ernie Townsend, my caretaker for more than 20 years, had wisely moved all the first floor furniture to the second floor before the storm hit. Chip Callaway, a landscape designer in Greensboro, North Carolina, then came to the garden's

rescue, designing and installing a totally new garden (much improved) on short notice. The magnolia trees and palms he installed were so large they had to be delivered at 4:00 A.M. when there was no traffic. The house also had to be completely repainted and rewired on the first floor since five feet of seawater came into the house during the hurricane. But all's well that ends well, and, as evident by his foreword to this book, His Royal Highness and accompanying entourage seemed to enjoy their stay at 9 East Battery, which by then showed few signs of Hugo.

While Roper House (the house, not me) seems to attract the rich and powerful when they come to Charleston and is wonderful for large parties, you don't have to have a lot of company—or any company—to enjoy this wonderful mansion. What could be nicer than sipping the obligatory bourbon (when back in the South, do as southerners do—drink bourbon and water) on the piazza with the tall columns framing a view of the ocean. Fragrant jasmine and pittosporum scent the breezes in spring, and the full moon never seems bigger to me than it does here, rising out of the Atlantic Ocean. I also like the house on warm summer evenings, when one feels the presence of the Old South. There are so many memories here, not just in this house but in Charleston itself with its 330-year history—including hurricanes, an earthquake and two wars fought right here. The past may be too much with us in Charleston, but sometimes it's nice to get away from our high-tech world. Charleston is the perfect place to escape to a kinder, gentler life.

The Roper House puts on quite a show for passersby when lights are blazing in all the tall, floor-length windows.

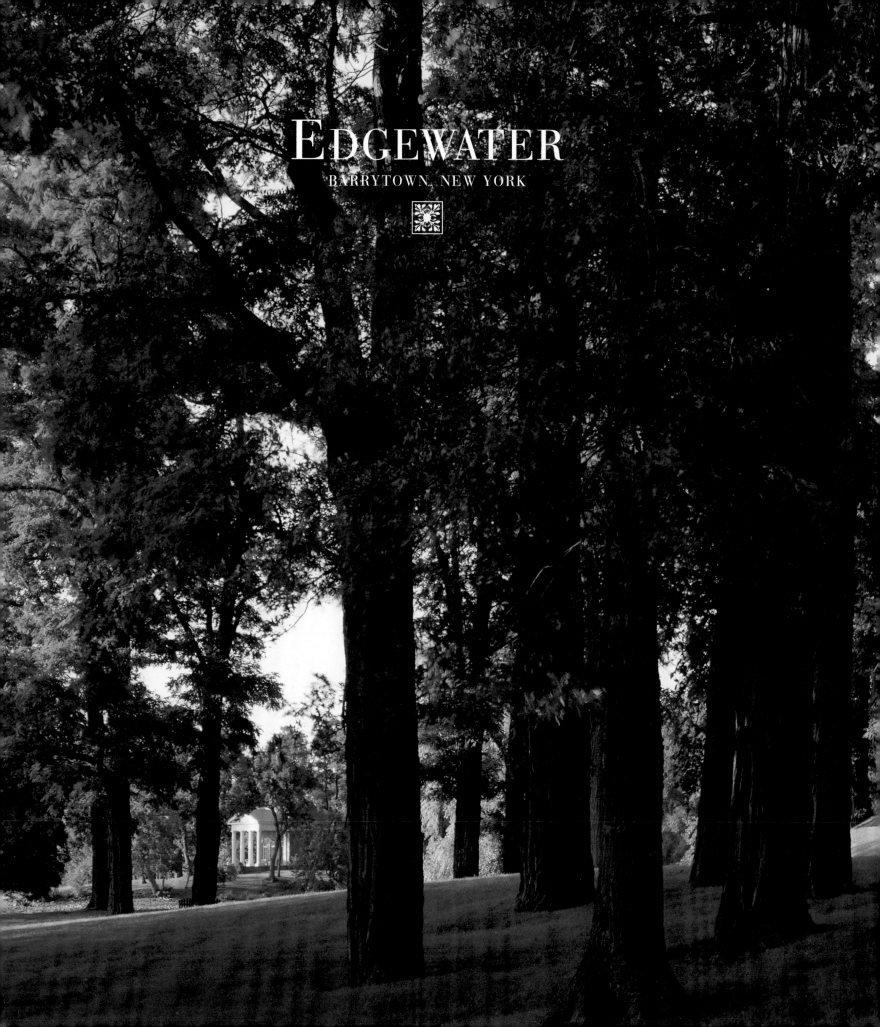

EDGEWATER

BARRYTOWN, NEW YORK

CHAPTER 9

EDGEWATER

Edgewater has been the great love of my life, architecturally speaking, since I first laid eyes on it thirty years ago. Well named because of its location, Edgewater is a handsome classical revival house built in 1820 on a small point of land jutting into the Hudson River in Barrytown, Dutchess County, New York. It is one of a number of "Livingston houses," built by or for members of the powerful Livingston family that once commanded vast stretches of the Hudson Valley. Less famous and smaller in scale than its neighboring Livingston houses—Montgomery Place and Clermont—Edgewater seems eminently more attractive and livable to me. But I am biased after twenty-nine years residence in what some might consider a museum, but which is home to me.

Why is Edgewater so seductive? First, I believe, is the site itself. The small peninsula on which the house is built is surrounded by placid lagoons, lined with weeping willows and ancient basswood trees drooping

(Preceding and left) The massive Doric columns at Edgewater, circa 1820, represent one of the earliest examples of the use of columns on residential buildings in America.

Even had it not been built on so dramatic a site, the classical architecture of Edgewater would make the house appealing in almost any setting.

into the river. The front porch of the house is no more than fifty yards from the edge of the river, making it possible to hear the lapping of the waves, sometimes gently, sometimes noisily. The Hudson is a mile wide and still tidal at this point, and the constant ebb and flow create a changing panorama of exposed rocks and rivulets when the tide is out.

Edgewater faces due west, with clear views of the Catskill Mountains except on foggy days, which also can be sublime in this setting. A greensward of lawn runs from the house to river's edge, reminding me that the place was once called "River Lawn," prior to a mid-nineteenth-century name change to Edgewater. Either is certainly appropriate to the setting. Sitting by the river's edge at sunset on long summer evenings is pure bliss.

Even had it not been built on so dramatic a site, the classical architecture of Edgewater would make the house appealing in almost any setting. The dominant feature is a massive pedimented colonnade—six Doric columns, two stories high—facing the river. Between the columns are five tall, arched French doors with fanlights at the top and shutters on the sides. Edgewater represents one of the earliest examples in the U.S. of the

The rear of Edgewater forms one side of a garden court with fountain. Tall weeping beeches and weeping hemlock create a romantic aura surrounding the garden.

(Right) My favorite place for lazy afternoons is this comfortable corner of the front porch, with its tall columns, a view across the Hudson River, and a glimpse of the new guest house.

use of columns on a domestic residence; previously such formal colonnades were reserved for public buildings, banks and institutions, but not residences. In this sense, Edgewater anticipated the coming Greek Revival mania that soon was to sweep American architecture for several decades until the Civil War.

The strict symmetry of Edgewater's original 1820 central block is offset by a handsome octagonal library, added by the architect A.J. Davis on the north side of

the house in 1854. At that time the entire structure was stuccoed a pinkish brown color and scored to resemble stone. A mid-nineteenth-century photograph now in my possession shows Edgewater with an elegant *faux marbre* façade, a treatment reproduced for me some years ago by Robert Jackson, who has marbleized so many walls for me over the years.

With the huge columns, arched doorways, and mellow brown façade, the overall effect of Edgewater is more Roman than Grecian. The house is very evocative of Palladio's mid-sixteenth-century villas built in the Italian Veneto along the Brenta Canal, especially Villa Malcontenta, with similar tall columns and a comparable location on a willow-lined bend in the Brenta near Venice. If Edgewater is not quite as grand as Malcontenta, the Brenta is no match for the mighty Hudson!

Edgewater is entered via the land side through a much smaller columned portico, thereby keeping the huge columns and large porch along the riverside as a dramatic surprise to visitors. The entrance door leads into a spacious hallway along the back side of the house, highlighted on the left by a grand spiral staircase circling two flights up to the bedroom floor and beyond to a full attic floor (now used as a library). To the right of the entrance is a small reception room, possibly used as an office in early days, although the bright red color of the walls—the original color found under many layers of paint—suggests something more amusing than an office.

Edgewater is entered from the back side through this impressive stair hall. The painted floor by Robert Jackson is copied from an inlaid floor I admired in Russia's Hermitage Palace in St. Petersburg.

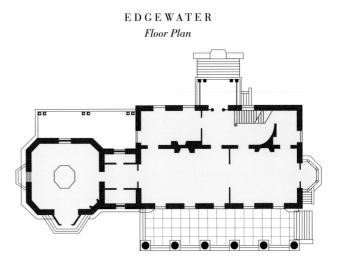

EDGEWATER
Floor Plan

Moving directly through the hallway from the front door, one enters a handsome suite of two connecting rooms along the river. The larger of the two is the living room, with three of the tall arched French doors opening onto the porch. The smaller, to the left, with two of the arched French doors, is the dining room. Sliding mahogany double doors between the living room and dining room make it possible to throw the two rooms together *en suite*. When the French doors are open to the porch on mild days, both porch and interior rooms flow together as a unified whole—a great place for a party! The ceilings inside are fourteen feet high, and all the original late Federal-style moldings, medallions, mantels, and mahogany doors have somehow survived the house's 180-year history.

The entrance to the Octagon Library, added later to the north side of the house, is on an axis with the living room and dining room, creating an attractive *enfilade* of rooms in the best European manner. The Octagon Library itself provides an architectural shock effect to visitors. One enters through a small, comparatively low-ceilinged connecting hall. Then the surprise: twenty-six-foot-high ceilings, soaring upward from the eight sides to

a central octagonal skylight, flooding the room with light. Huge arched doorways on all sides provide further vistas of river and gardens beyond. I always want to say "WOW" when I enter this magnificent space, even though I have lived here nearly thirty years.

Edgewater is larger than it appears to be from the outside. The second floor includes two huge bedrooms along the riverside and a smaller guest room overlooking the hills behind Edgewater. The attic, built into the triangular pediment over the front columns, conceals a full third floor—mostly a library of more than 10,000 books (no one lacks reading material at Edgewater) and another guest room. Then at ground level there is also a full basement floor, with the original kitchen (recently restored), a large dining room and servants quarters. Because the principal floor of Edgewater is built high above ground level, the basement is well lit by large triple windows which repeat the architectural fenestration of the upper two floors. Thus, Edgewater contains four full floors of usable space even though it is built to look like a two-story house.

Before moving on to Edgewater's quite interesting history, let me tell you how I came to own this jewel of a house and site. It seemed like fate had intended me to have it. On a warm late September afternoon in 1969, I had been touring old houses of the Hudson Valley with Bill Thompson, a friend who shares my love of old houses. We had just taken a look at Maizefield, an old

A portrait of Robert Donaldson, painted by Charles Robert Leslie in 1821, surveys the dining room at Edgewater, with its suite of Duncan Phyfe chairs and French porcelain, all once owned by the Livingstons.

mansion in nearby Red Hook. The book we were using as a guide, *Great Houses of the Hudson Valley* by Eberlein, described another historic house (Edgewater) which was only a mile or two distant, due west and right on the river. The book showed a less than flattering photograph of a colonnaded house that looked vaguely southern in origin. The book noted that the current owner of Edgewater was the author Gore Vidal.

Although neither of us knew Gore Vidal, and the hour was late, we proceeded to the site, arriving at sunset. We looked down a long driveway following the river's edge and glimpsed Edgewater with its tall columns gleaming in the late afternoon sun. It was a magical view, with the water gently lapping the banks, shimmering light reflected off the river, and everything a lush green. The only intrusion into what otherwise seemed to be an earthly paradise was the presence of railroad tracks just east to the back of the property, but I have found in this life that nothing is ever completely perfect. In any event, I thought to myself, "What a perfect Shangri-La for a writer. I'll bet Gore Vidal would never sell this place."

Nor was I looking to buy another house, since I had just bought the Roper House as a second home in Charleston, South Carolina, the previous year. But I certainly coveted Edgewater from the moment I saw it; it looked so blissfully peaceful and I felt instantly at home there. It was also more accessible than the South

Edgewater's much admired drawing room, with three tall French doors opening to the river, features a pair of Albany, N.Y. mirrors, matching pier tables and Duncan Phyfe furniture. The white silk window hangings were installed by Anthony Hail 30 years ago when I first bought Edgewater.

Carolina house, since I worked only ninety miles away in New York City.

I returned to New York, but was unable to put Edgewater out of my mind. It seemed so perfect, a jewel set on the Hudson. Then came the telephone call from Anthony Hail with the news that Gore Vidal wanted to sell the house. To make a long story short, Tony told me how to contact Vidal in Italy, and three days later I had negotiated a deal to buy Edgewater, practically sight unseen. I've never regretted it, though I'm told by mutual friends that Gore later regretted selling it. However, he now has another Edgewater, high on the Amalfi coast of Italy overlooking the blue Mediterranean, so weep not for his loss. I hear his place is spectacular.

Gore Vidal has only returned to Edgewater one time since selling it to me in 1969. He had owned Edgewater for approximately twenty years, having bought it shortly after the end of World War II. During the war, I am told the double-tracked railroads right behind Edgewater were so busy shipping war supplies to the port of New York that Edgewater had become unlivable because of soot and noise. At that time, trains still belched coal smoke. The house had stood empty during the war years. President Franklin Delano Roosevelt used to like to come up from Hyde Park and sit on the front porch of deserted Edgewater (with a favorite cousin, Daisy Suckley) to watch the sunsets on the

This is the original red color we found buried under many layers of paint in this small reception room off the entrance hall. The harp belonged to Mrs. Robert Donaldson and the unusual sofa is by Duncan Phyfe and probably was custom-made for Robert Donaldson in 1820.

Hudson. Perhaps FDR was able to command the trains to stop for awhile.

Under Gore Vidal's post-World War II aegis, Edgewater revived and had a colorful 20-year era of fun and literature. Gore called the place "Edgewater U" because he advanced his education there while writing and apparently enjoying himself. On one or more occasions, Eleanor Roosevelt evidently also discovered the charms of Edgewater while visiting Vidal, who enjoyed a fascinating coterie of friends, including such regulars as Paul Newman and Joanne Woodward. (For readers interested in learning more about the Vidal years at Edgewater, I refer you to Gore's autobiography, *Palimpsest*, published by Random House in 1997, replete with details of his seemingly very happy years at Edgewater.)

For at least a decade after I bought Edgewater, locals (on learning where I lived) said "Oh, you have Gore Vidal's house." I think a lot of Gore Vidal must still be at Edgewater. His biography indicated that he sometimes still dreams of the place. I have all his published works in Edgewater's Octagon Library, where he did his writing. There must be something contagious in that room. I have produced this book, as well as an earlier book, *The Contrarian Manager*, about my business career. Both were written in large part in the same library that Vidal used.

The spectacular Octagon Library, designed by Alexander Jackson Davis, was added to the north side of Edgewater in the early 1850s. Robert Donaldson called it his "sanctum sanctorum." The unusual carpet design was copied from a ceiling in the Roman Baths of Pompeii.

Let's move back in time to the beginning of Edgewater as a Hudson River estate. The land on which Edgewater was built was owned by John R. Livingston, one of the patriarchs of the Livingston clan that dominated the Hudson Valley for much of the eighteenth and nineteenth centuries. I have a copy of the original deed conveying the property in 1820 from John R. Livingston to his daughter Margaretta Livingston Brown, who had recently married Captain Lowndes Brown, a descendant of a prominent southern family in Charleston, South Carolina. This was one of four marriages between the Livingstons of New York and members of the Lowndes family of Charleston. There is strong circumstantial evidence that Robert Mills, a nationally recognized architect from Charleston, drew the original plans for Edgewater. It has all the hallmarks of houses Mills designed in South Carolina in the 1820s. That would explain the strongly southern character of the house: high ceilings, huge windows, raised piazza above the ground level, as in Charleston. None of these traits are particularly well-suited to a colder northern climate. Since I had just bought Roper House in Charleston, this added another taste of predestination that this house was meant for me.

The Lowndes Browns apparently had an idyllic life at their classically styled villa on the Hudson. This was before the railroad severed the peninsula, on which the house was built, from the rolling hills behind. In 1852, some thirty years after the house was built, Mrs. Brown's world seemed to come crashing down. Her influential father, John R. Livingston, died at age ninety-six. I suppose that could not have been a total surprise. But her husband Lowndes Brown also died in the same year. The third blow to Mrs. Brown that year was the building of the railroad on land, taken against her will by New York State through eminent domain procedures, right behind her beautiful home (no more than twenty-five yards away). One can only surmise whether apoplexy over the coming of the railroad had anything to do with the deaths of both John R. Livingston and Lowndes Brown in that year. In any event, Mrs. Brown had had enough. She sold the house and moved to London (where her only daughter had married the Belgian ambassador to the Court of St. James), vowing never to return to the U.S., so angry was she at the railroad. She is buried in Kensal Green in London.

Not too much remains from the Lowndes Brown era at Edgewater, in part because the next owner, Robert Donaldson, was so vigorous in planting his own imprint on the property. Donaldson was a wealthy, transplanted North Carolinian who purchased the property from the widow Brown in 1852. Before that he had created and owned Blithewood, a nearby Hudson River estate famed for its picturesque landscape and now a part of the Bard College campus. Donaldson was born and raised in Fayetteville, North Carolina—another coincidence for me since my hometown of Raleigh, North Carolina is only fifty miles away. At age twenty-one, Donaldson had inherited $300,000 from a bachelor uncle in London, a vast sum in 1820 (The coincidence with my life stopped there; I had no rich uncle!). Donaldson's wife, Susan Gaston Donaldson, was a North Carolinian

This is my inevitable "blue heaven" bedroom (I've used the same bedroom color scheme in most of my houses in order to feel "at home"—in bed at least!). The windows have great views of the Hudson River.

from New Bern, also close enough to my birthplace to give me a feeling of kinship. Other parallels between my life and Robert Donaldson—130 years apart—included the fact that we both were graduates of the University of North Carolina, both of us migrated to New York in our twenties, we both served as Trustees of New York University, we both were intensely interested in art and architecture, and, finally, the name of my investment firm in New York just happened to be *Donaldson,*

The north bedroom at Edgewater is enlivened by cheerful peach, gold and green hangings at bed and windows. The carpet is a replica of one shown in a portrait of President Monroe at City Hall in New York.

Lufkin & Jenrette. Of course, I knew none of this at the time I bought Edgewater; the Donaldson connection all came out later. It all seemed a bit eerie and almost preordained when I later discovered these ties, as well as the strange way I had found the house. It rather seemed like the house had found me.

Other similarly "miraculous" occurrences, once I had discovered the Donaldsons' history so similar to mine, made it seem like some divine hand up there was planning it all. Almost miraculously, the Donaldson furnishings began to return to Edgewater. First was a life-size portrait of Mrs. Donaldson which came to my attention through an *ANTIQUES* magazine article on the artist George Cook. This eventually led to my obtaining not only the portrait but a sofa and a pair of window benches by Duncan Phyfe that had belonged to the Donaldsons. Then I learned that the Colonial Dames of New York owned the harp that Mrs. Donaldson was shown playing in her portrait—but how to retrieve it? The Dames did not want to sell. Weeks later I noticed an *identical* harp coming up for sale at Sotheby's, which seemed almost miraculous. This time the Dames agreed to swap me their harp for this one, which I proceeded to buy at Sotheby's. So Mrs. Donaldson's original harp is back at Edgewater standing next to her portrait, which shows the harp's details clearly. Mrs. Donaldson was quite proficient musically, and I keep awaiting ghostly tunes at night.

Caught up in the spirit of things (so to speak), I decided to be more pro-active. John Sanders, a friend and college mate of mine in North Carolina, had been concurrently researching Robert Donaldson's life (I suppose yet another coincidence). I learned from John that Donaldson had been a great friend and patron of Alexander Jackson Davis, one of the nation's most famous architects at the time, who had been instrumental in building the North Carolina State Capitol, in Raleigh, as well as many other buildings at the University of North Carolina. Donaldson had been largely responsible for A. J. Davis receiving these important commissions in North Carolina. My feeling of "connectedness" with this man, Robert Donaldson, was growing by leaps and bounds.

John Sanders told me that the last living descendant of Robert Donaldson—his great-granddaughter Mary Cromwell Allison—was now residing in Spain on the Costa del Sol. So, on a chance, I wrote Mrs. Allison and told her I was restoring Edgewater, her family's ancestral home. She promptly invited me to visit her the next time I was in Europe. I soon found an excuse to go to Spain, and this time I really hit the jackpot. Greeting me as I entered her house was a marvelous portrait of Robert Donaldson himself, smiling an enigmatic Mona Lisa smile now that I had found him. I learned that the portrait was painted in London in 1821 by Charles Robert Leslie, an American artist, right after Donaldson had collected his inheritance (a more likely cause of his smile than my arrival to rescue him from Spain). Mary Allison's house was chock-full of other Donaldson treasures and memorabilia: a grandfather clock, wine cellarette, chairs, family silver, some other family portraits, and photographs. All had been at Edgewater in the last half of the nineteenth century.

Although we had a cordial visit and established correspondence, Mrs. Allison was unwilling to part with any of her family possessions (her only connection to home), but she said, in the presence of her husband, that she would like all these things to return to Edgewater some day after her death (she had no living family members to inherit them). Mary Allison had been in poor health at the time, and

*Michael Dwyer designed this Palladian-style guest
house on a point of land across the water from Edgewater.
It was built, almost single-handedly, by Michael
Pelletier in 1997-98.*

several years later she passed away. To my surprise,
her husband, Ivor Allison, contacted me and said,
"Mary had wanted her Donaldson family things to go
back to Edgewater. Come and get them!" And so I did.
Robert Donaldson's portrait is now reunited with that
of his wife, with the *tout ensemble* creating quite a
history of the Donaldson era at Edgewater.

If you want to learn more about the quite interesting
Donaldson years at Edgewater, I recommend that you
purchase *Carolinian on the Hudson: the Life of Robert
Donaldson*, published by The Historic Preservation
Foundation of North Carolina, Inc., in Raleigh. Jean
Bradley Anderson, the author, did an outstanding job of
researching and bringing to life Robert Donaldson's

extraordinary career, both as a transplanted "taste
maker" exporting fashionable New York taste to then
rural North Carolina and as an *arbiter elegantiarum*, a
title bestowed on Donaldson by A.J. Downing, renowned
for his picturesque landscaping in the Hudson Valley
and books on horticulture. *Carolinian on the Hudson*
gives an authentic view of the rather idyllic life along the
Hudson during the mid-nineteenth century before the
Civil War splintered the nation.

The "three-D" trinity of Robert Donaldson (the
wealthy patron), A. J. Davis (the architect), and
A. J. Downing (landscaping) were the reigning
tastemakers of the Hudson Valley in the mid-nineteenth
century. Donaldson also maintained close friendships
with the Hudson River school artists, including Asher
Durand, Thomas Cole and Samuel F. B. Morse, all of
whom visited the Donaldsons at Edgewater or their
previous home, Blithewood. A.J. Davis, at Donaldson's
behest, designed the charming octagonal library, added
to Edgewater in 1854, along with a pair of octagonal
gate houses, tenant houses, and other ornamental
structures on the Edgewater grounds.

Robert Donaldson died at Edgewater in 1872 (his
wife predeceased him in 1866), but his children
continued to live at Edgewater until 1902 (completing
fifty years of Donaldson ownership), at which point it
was sold to the John Jay Chapmans. Chapman was
another popular literary figure, preceding Vidal at
Edgewater. Mrs. Chapman was one of the famed "Astor
orphans" of nearby Rokeby. The Chapmans owned
Edgewater for about forty years but made their principal
home at Sylvania, which they built in the early twentieth
century on high ground overlooking the Hudson on part
of the old Donaldson estate. This house has recently been

lovingly restored by Adam and Joan Lerrick, making a charming companion house to Edgewater.

After the Chapmans moved to Sylvania, Edgewater languished, unloved and unlived-in for most of the next forty years, including the Depression years and the noisy coal-burning railroad heyday of World War II, until it was rescued by Gore Vidal after the war's end. The coming of quieter, less smelly and dirty diesel locomotives, together with less traffic after the war,

The interior of my new guest house echoes the architecture of Edgewater.

made Edgewater once again habitable. Its charming location on the river and elegant architecture made it worth putting up with the occasional train rushing by. Alan Porter, a neighbor, used to tell this tale about Gore Vidal's dinner parties: As usual, Gore, the reigning

intellectual, dominated dinner table conversation at Edgewater. When he heard a train coming, he would turn to the guest next to him and say, "Now tell me about your life." Just as the person began to talk, the train would roar by, drowning out all conversation. Once the train had passed, Gore would resume his dominance over the conversation. I always recall this line, "Now tell me about your life!" when a train rushes by during one of my dinner parties at Edgewater.

Today, mostly passenger trains between New York and Albany run on the tracks behind Edgewater. They go by quickly every hour or so and aren't really so objectionable. I've planted the tracks out visually. Still, the railroad remains a sort of Sword of Damocles hanging over Edgewater if the tracks were ever converted to longer, noisier freight trains. Well, there's always a serpent lurking in the Garden of Eden, it seems.

As you may gather from this essay, my nearly thirty years at Edgewater have been a delight. Much of what I have done to the old place has been in the nature of restoring it to its original elegance. In addition to the Donaldson family furnishings which returned so mysteriously, I have filled the house with antiques and *objets d'art* of the early nineteenth century, contemporary with the construction of the house in 1820. The drawing room has an unusual suite of late Federal-style (1815-20) Duncan Phyfe furniture, including a sofa and four side chairs all with rare curule form legs, said to be copied from chairs used by Roman senators. In the dining room, I was able to acquire a rare suite of twelve Duncan Phyfe dining chairs which formerly belonged to the Livingstons. These chairs, arguably the finest Phyfe ever made, are unusually heavy and of great strength and elegance. I acquired

The new pool house was also designed by Michael Dwyer and built by Michael Pelletier in 1998. The pool is deliberately hidden by a slight rise in the lawn.

(Left) The fountain courtyard behind Edgewater provides a cool retreat from the hot afternoon sun reflected off the river.

them from the estate of the late Edward Vason Jones. The dining room is also filled with Livingston-owned *Porcelaine de Paris*, each piece gold-stamped with the Livingston "L," which I acquired at auction many years ago from one of the Hudson River estates. Also from the Livingston era is a fanciful portrait by John Vanderlyn of Julia Livingston (sister of Edgewater's first owner, Margaret Livingston Brown) shown dancing in the gardens of Massena. As I think back over my inventory of furnishings and *objets d'art* at Edgewater, I am surprised by how many Livingston, as well as Donaldson, things have found their way back to the old home place.

Gilbert Stuart painted these two portraits of Marcia Burns Van Ness and her husband Gen. John Peter Van Ness. They became separated at least seventy years ago, but are now reunited at Edgewater.

By no means are all the furnishings now at Edgewater related to these two families, and many came to me through equally unusual circumstances. For example, I acquired an early-nineteenth-century portrait of General John Peter Van Ness, painted by Gilbert Stuart, from members of the Van Ness family, long-time residents of nearby Columbia County, New York. Van Ness was elected a congressman from the area and, as an eligible bachelor, wooed and won the hand of Marcia Burns, daughter of Davy Burns, a Scotsman who owned much of the land on which present Washington, D.C., including the White House, is built. Van Ness later became the first mayor of Washington, D. C.

I always suspected there must have been a mate to this portrait of General Van Ness. Once again, fate intervened. A story on Edgewater in *Town & Country* showed the portrait of General Van Ness in the background of one of the rooms. Shortly thereafter, I received a letter from another Van Ness descendant (in Baltimore), advising me that she had seen the article and wanted me to know that she owned the mate to the Gilbert Stuart portrait of Van Ness that I owned. So I hot-footed my way to Baltimore and there was the portrait of Marcia Burns Van Ness: seated in an identical chair as her husband, but facing him—same olive background color, same frame, etc. We calculated that the two portraits had been separated for at least seventy years. It took me a few more years to buy Marcia's

The rear courtyard evokes a Roman atrium feeling, with a bust of Julius Caesar, obelisks, and urns. The wall and lush greenery conceal the double tracks of the railroad, which runs behind Edgewater.

Late fall brings the most spectacular sunsets on the Hudson at Edgewater.

portrait, but the two are now happily reunited in the living room at Edgewater. This is only one of several cases in which I have been able to match up pier tables, card tables, etc. with identical pieces, usually found years later. Such is the joy of collecting antiques!

In recent years, I've begun to make more of my own architectural imprint on the Edgewater property. This past year I added a small neo-classical guest house, built on a point of land across the lagoon to the north of

Edgewater—far enough away not to compete with the main house. Designed by Michael Dwyer of New York, the guest house is a small Grecian temple with four columns on the Doric order framing a large porch looking downriver. Viewed from the front porch of

Edgewater across the lagoon, the new structure serves as an architectural folly extending the sweep of landscape to the north. On the far south side of the Edgewater grounds, Michael Dwyer also relocated the swimming pool and added a charming pool house, again in classical style with four Doric columns along the side of the pool. The effect is quite Roman—rather like a small corner of Hadrian's Villa. From guest house to pool house and back to the main house provides a scenic one-mile roundabout walk, mostly along the winding riverbank.

I am also having fun landscaping the large acreage I own on the opposite side of the railroad tracks. I've hidden the railroad by a low arborvitae screen (I got this idea from Robert Donaldson who mentioned his "arborvitae screen along the railroad" in a letter to A.J. Davis.). Beyond the tracks the hillside slopes upward to form a natural bowl. I've kept the meadows mostly in lawn and clumps of trees in my version of an English "Capability Brown" landscape. I should perhaps call this area the Deer Park, since early morning and evening bring scores of deer grazing and racing across the open hillside. From the top of these hills (at a place I call Nirvana Point) one can look back, westward across the Hudson River to a perfect, unobstructed view of the Catskill Mountains, seen much the way the Hudson River school of artists would have seen them 150 years ago.

Often when I am alone at Edgewater, I feel like I should be sharing the beauty of the house and grounds with others. I try not to be selfish, and I open it frequently to tour groups, including preservation groups, garden clubs, history buffs, architects, etc. The proximity to New York City also makes the place accessible to friends. Unfortunately, I can't accommodate all requests for tours or I'd never be able to use Edgewater myself, and Jack Smith, my indispensable manager for the past twenty years, would have to become a full-time tour guide.

The biggest social event at Edgewater during my era was a spectacular twenty-fifth anniversary party for Donaldson, Lufkin & Jenrette in 1984. Turning a problem (the railroad) into an opportunity, we chartered a private train that brought 400 guests from Grand Central Station (where we had laid out a red carpet) to the very back door of Edgewater. The train was turned around at Albany and returned late in the evening to pick up the celebrants after a dinner-dance on the lawn and a fireworks grand finale over the river. All my subsequent entertainments have paled in comparison.

From mid-May to late October, when the brilliant fall foliage finally departs, there is no place I'd rather be than Edgewater. Probably I should come up more often in winter, when spectacular sunsets on the frozen Hudson and cozy fires in the fireplaces (each room has one) have a different sort of charm. But whenever I return to Edgewater, I am always reminded of a passage from a diary kept by Robert Donaldson as a young man of eighteen years. Donaldson and some Chapel Hill classmates had taken a trip from North Carolina to "the Canadas" in 1818. They returned by sailing down the Hudson River on a moonlit evening. As they neared New York and found the river lined with handsome villas, Donaldson wrote in his diary "Thought it the consummation of earthly bliss to live in one of those pallaces on such a noble river, under such a government." He got his wish twenty years later. It's also just the way I feel 180 years later: life at Edgewater is the consummation of earthly bliss!

Ayr Mount

Hillsborough, North Carolina

CHAPTER 10

AYR MOUNT

Unlike my other houses with their imposing colonnades and classical motifs, "the grandeur that was Rome" is nowhere to be found at Ayr Mount, a much simpler but handsome Federal-period brick house built in 1814-16 by William Kirkland near Hillsborough, North Carolina. Yet the house has a great feeling of antiquity and timelessness, almost lost in time and haunted by 170 years of occupancy by Kirkland's descendants, many of whom rest in an adjoining family cemetery. With the old house largely unchanged and many of its original furnishings intact, a visit to Ayr Mount tells much about the history of North Carolina and the early republic. Since I have given Ayr Mount to Classical American Homes Preservation Trust, the house and grounds are now open to the public under the auspices of Preservation North Carolina, a state historic preservation organization.

When I bought Ayr Mount in 1985 from the nephew of the widow of the last living Kirkland descendant,

The house has a great feeling of antiquity and timelessness, almost lost in time and haunted by 170 years of occupancy by Kirkland's descendants, many of whom rest in an adjoining family cemetery.

(Preceding and left) The austere brick façade of William Kirkland's great house became the prototype of North Carolina architecture, which has always been simpler than in neighboring Virginia and South Carolina.

I had no such thoughts of turning Ayr Mount into a house museum—at least not for many years. Rather, I saw it as a semi-retirement home of sorts in my native North Carolina. After selling Donaldson, Lufkin & Jenrette to The Equitable earlier that year, I briefly contemplated a return to academia—as a student, professor, or administrator—leaving the roller coaster of Wall Street behind. In this respect Ayr Mount was strategically located, a secluded country home almost equidistant from Duke University, nine miles to the east, and the University of North Carolina at Chapel Hill, ten miles southeast. Ayr Mount was also close to Raleigh, my hometown, where I still had many friends despite thirty years living in New York City.

But it was not to be. Shortly after I bought Ayr Mount, Equitable asked me to stay on as chairman of the board, dashing any thoughts of a return to academia. One thing led to another, and ten years later I was still hard at work in New York. Meanwhile, I had also acquired Cane Garden in the Virgin Islands and Millford Plantation in South Carolina. I was visiting Ayr Mount so rarely that it seemed a shame to have such an extraordinary house and setting sit there unused. Yet I loved the house and had put so much love and care, to say nothing of money,

The Kirklands' elegant Broadwood fortepiano appears always to have been in the West Parlor, perhaps used as a music room.

A portrait and bust of Thomas Jefferson survey the all-white West Parlor. Note the unusual Gothic cornice around the ceiling and the high wainscoting.

into its restoration that I could not bear to sell it, thereby losing this important link to North Carolina history. Then a light bulb went on somewhere, and presto, Classical American Homes Preservation Trust was founded to own not only Ayr Mount, but in time some or all of my other historic houses, eventually making them available for public visitation. Even though Ayr Mount is now in the public domain as a house museum, it remains

This portrait of Judge William Gaston, which once hung at Edgewater, descended in the family of William Kirkland, whose grandson married Gaston's granddaughter.

Ayr Mount's bright and cheery East wing was probably William and Margaret Kirkland's bedroom when the house was first built. In later years it was used as a dining room. It now serves as an office, with comfortable chairs for relaxing. Bust is of Judge Gaston.

one of my pet projects. I'm having just as much fun with Ayr Mount finding ways to share it with others.

Like all of my other houses, I stumbled upon Ayr Mount by accident. John Sanders, who played a seminal role in helping me track down the last living descendant of Robert Donaldson of Edgewater (thereby leading to the return of many of the original Donaldson furnishings),

AYR MOUNT
Floor Plan

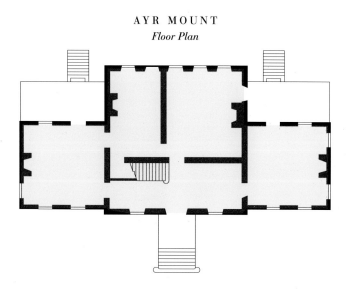

was again the instrument (or guide) that led me to Ayr Mount. I had gone to Chapel Hill to deliver a speech when Sanders, whose keen legal mind is equally adept when it comes to art and architecture—especially anything related to North Carolina and its state capitol—suggested that we visit Ayr Mount in nearby Hillsborough. While I certainly did not need another house (I had three at the time), I have learned to listen carefully when John Sanders says a house or *objet d'art* is interesting. So off we went, ostensibly just to look at Ayr Mount. But when I drove onto the grounds and entered the old house, so typical of the best of early North Carolina architecture and with the most unusual architectural woodwork I had ever seen in that region, I knew that I had to do something to rescue it. I had done very little before to help preserve great architecture in my home state, and I felt this was the time and place. And having just sold DLJ to Equitable, there was money in the bank for a change, in contrast to my other house purchases. The price also was right: $450,000 for this superbly intact Federal-period house on fifty-two acres of rolling North Carolina countryside in the heart of the booming Research Triangle.

With John Sanders as architectural historian, Todd Dickinson as my contractor, and Paul (Chip) Callaway as landscape advisor, we embarked upon a fascinating, if expensive, two-year program of restoring Ayr Mount to its original early-nineteenth-century state when William Kirkland built the house. No expense was spared. We were inspired in our efforts by a portrait of Kirkland himself that had never left its position of honor above the dining room fireplace mantel. His spirit continues to pervade the house, the great pride of the Kirkland family over the next 170 years.

A few notes on William Kirkland: Born in Ayr, Scotland, in 1768 of humble origins (his father was a butcher), Kirkland emigrated to America as a young man shortly after the American Revolution. He first appeared in North Carolina in 1789 as a clerk to a Scottish merchant in Warrenton. Three years later he moved to Hillsborough, establishing his own general store. The thrifty young Scot prospered and his business later expanded to include a tannery and a cotton gin, plus partnerships in general stores in other North Carolina towns. Although primarily a merchant, he also invested successfully in real estate, acquiring a large tract of land in Tennessee. Kirkland married Margaret Scott (the daughter of a former business partner) in 1792 and their family grew—ultimately to 14 children, of whom two sons and eight daughters reached maturity. In 1799 he purchased 503 acres one mile east of Hillsborough, which

The large center room was used originally as the family dining room. The portrait of William Kirkland, by Jacob Marling, has never left its place of honor over the mantel in Ayr Mount's 185-year history.

became the site of present-day Ayr Mount. Aside from the needs of his burgeoning family, the inspiration to build Ayr Mount appeared to come from a long-delayed trip Kirkland made to his native Scotland in 1811 and 1812 to renew his family ties after a twenty-year absence. The evident financial success and social prominence that had been achieved by some members of his family in London and Scotland undoubtedly encouraged Kirkland, upon his return to America, to build a fine house that would reflect his own success and standing in the community. And so, in 1814, shortly after the termination of hostilities in the War of 1812, Kirkland began construction of Ayr Mount, which he named in honor of his home place in Scotland.

Ayr Mount remained in the Kirkland family for four generations. Five of William Kirkland's eight daughters married (one son-in-law became chief justice of the North Carolina Supreme Court and another a U.S. senator). Both sons married women who were related to North Carolina's then richest families.

William Kirkland's own fortune began to wane in the late 1820s, in part through what proved to be imprudent guarantees of loans by business partners and relatives. He died in 1836, on the eve of the financial panic of 1837 which set the region and entire nation back for a decade. The house was acquired by John Umstead Kirkland, the eldest son and executor. While

Another view of the dining room, including the Kirklands' original table. The large classical mirror reflects an unusual built-in mahogany and glazed cupboard for displaying china and glassware. The portraits of two Virginia gentlemen are by John Wollaston.

Ayr Mount seems to have been spruced up considerably in the 1850s when John Umstead Kirkland's wife came into her inheritance, the Civil War soon put a stop to this brief respite from hard times. The war, of course, was followed by the poverty of Reconstruction in the South, and the Kirklands struggled to hold on to Ayr Mount itself, although much of the surrounding acreage was sold in order to save the house.

The fourth generation of Kirklands, born in the aftermath of the Civil War and enduring two world wars and the 1930s Depression, seemed to have had the most difficulty in maintaining Ayr Mount and lived reclusive lives. As John Sanders noted in an article on Ayr Mount in *ANTIQUES* Magazine, "the Kirklands seem to have been as much possessed by the house as they possessed it." Of seven children, only two married (both late in life) and there were no children from either marriage. And so, Ayr Mount passed into non-family hands—mine.

Ayr Mount today has been returned to its original pristine condition. When I go there I sometimes wonder how I could have given up such a handsome place to live, in such an attractive setting, but I truly believe this is a house, with its rich legacy from the past, that belongs in the public domain. A visit to Ayr Mount today is like turning the clock back 185 years.

The house is attractively situated on a high ridge of land overlooking the Eno River Valley, just east of Hillsborough, which itself is a veritable cornucopia of late-eighteenth- and early-nineteenth-century architecture. Ayr Mount is just far enough removed from town to evoke a rare "country feeling" in the rapidly growing Raleigh-Durham-Chapel Hill Research Triangle area. Recently, with the assistance of Preservation North Carolina and the James Johnston

Trust, Classical American Homes Preservation Trust was able to acquire more land on the opposite side of the Eno River, protecting Ayr Mount's viewscape to the opposing ridge line on the south side of the river. With this land and earlier purchases, the Ayr Mount tract has now grown to 265 acres, about half the size of William Kirkland's original tract. Together with my neighbors' adjoining gardens and land on which preservation easements have recently been donated to a land conservancy, we have an incredible nature preserve that includes several miles of wild woodlands, along the winding Eno River, that should be safe for posterity (despite the desire of some highway planners to run a new four-lane highway along the eastern perimeter of Ayr Mount). Currently, we are installing nature trails which will be open without charge to the public.

Ayr Mount today is well hidden from noisy public roads. The house was built facing the old Halifax Road, the major artery to the north from Hillsborough. In this case North Carolina's highway planners many years ago unwittingly enhanced Ayr Mount's solitude by relocating this highway about one hundred yards to the north, away from the house. The driveway into Ayr Mount now sneaks almost invisibly off this road between two suburban homes, one of which I acquired as a caretaker's house. The gates of Ayr Mount stand on the long unused old Halifax Road, which has become nothing more than a romantic trace.

Adding to the romance, this part of the Halifax Road in front of Ayr Mount is believed to have followed the old Indian Trading Path, a famous trail developed by Native Americans—leading west to Cherokee lands— for transport between the Roanoke River, which drains much of the lower half of Virginia, and tributaries near present-day Charlotte which run into the Santee River, South Carolina's mightiest river. The Trading Path, probably North Carolina's first road to the back country, facilitated transfer of goods between the water transportation provided by these two huge river systems. The Occaneechi Indians, who resided in the Hillsborough area, were among the foremost users, renowned as reliable carriers of merchandise between the two great rivers. A parcel of Ayr Mount's land—known as the Oxbow because of a hook in the Eno River—is believed to have been the site of some of the Occaneechi villages. For at least a decade, archeologists at the University of North Carolina have been exploring the Oxbow and have uncovered traces of several village sites.

In any event, the old deserted Halifax Road running in front of Ayr Mount today probably *looks* very much like the old Indian Trading Path would have looked. It is exciting to me to think about the key role this route played in opening up North Carolina. Even today, the most-used highway (I-85) and the most populous cities of North Carolina follow the crescent formed by the Indian Trading Path. The route is identified today by historical markers across the state.

William Kirkland wanted to make a statement about the growing prominence of his family when he built Ayr Mount in 1814-16. This house, one of the first to be built of brick in the area, faces north, back about one hundred yards from the old Halifax Road. It was approached from the road by a long, straight driveway running directly to the front door, thereby displaying the

A double-width Massachusetts gentleman's secretary-bookcase, circa 1800, anchors one side of the West Parlor.

strict symmetry of Ayr Mount's façade. The front lawn, on either side of the drive, was known as The Green. It would have been the center of polite gatherings by the Kirklands and their guests (The back side of Ayr Mount apparently was a work area, including a detached kitchen, dairy, smokehouse, corncrib, some slave houses, and barns.). On either side of The Green today, I have planted boxwoods which, after fourteen years of even slow boxwood growth, have created an enclosed area of green lawn where one wants to play croquet or simply frolic. Beyond the boxwoods are meadows, also kept well groomed, extending to distant forests on all sides.

Since the rear area of Ayr Mount has long since lost its outbuildings, or dependencies, I have opened up long vistas, running 300 yards or so downhill to the Eno River—usually a placid stream, though on one occasion I witnessed it flood to Mississippi-like proportions after a major storm. To the southeast is a wonderful unobstructed vista to Poplar Ridge, two miles distant across the Eno Valley. A small pond on the back side of Ayr Mount, originally for the use of grazing cattle or horses, has been enlarged by me to create a reflecting pond. From its far side one has a reflected view of the south facade of Ayr Mount. When the full moon rises in the valley to the left of Poplar Ridge and is reflected in the pond's waters, the setting is incredibly romantic.

David Byers decided I had too many blue bedrooms and designed these handsome Chinese Chippendale hangings in a bright pinkish-red color. This spacious bedroom on the second floor may have had at least two if not three double beds when the Kirklands' large family lived here.

Another bedroom on the second floor is enlivened by peach, yellow and green striped silk at the windows and bed, by David Byers. All woodwork has original paint color.

Indeed, now that Ayr Mount is open to the public, this has become a favorite site for weddings and receptions. Despite the population growth in this area, Ayr Mount remains an oasis of quiet. The feeling of timelessness is all-pervading, especially with night sounds of crickets and frogs and the old house seen by moonlight.

What about the house itself, which I have acknowledged is no Grecian or Roman temple? For its time and place, Ayr Mount was a fine, even grand house. The house was built on what has been called a tripartite plan, distantly Palladian in origin, that was popular in Virginia and eastern North Carolina in the late eighteenth and early nineteenth centuries. The plan consists of a two-story central block flanked by connecting one-story wings. Within the central block, a transverse passage hall along the front gives access to the principal rooms behind it and to the wings on either end. The transverse hall also contains a stairway to the second floor of the central block. At Ayr Mount, the stairway continues on to the third, or attic, floor.

From afar, Ayr Mount looks comfortable but not large. What is surprising when one approaches and enters the house is the large scale of the rooms.

The ceiling heights approach thirteen feet throughout the first floor and are only slightly lower on the second. The two flanking wings are each twenty-four feet square, light and airy, with windows on three sides. The one to the west has the more elegant woodwork and would have been the principal drawing room or music room. The somewhat simpler east wing might have been a master bedroom or office. The two-and-one-half-story central block has the usual transverse hall, this one large enough for dancing—perhaps the family's ballroom as well as a cool place on the north side of the house for the family to congregate. Behind the transverse hall are two rooms, including the largest room in the house—24 ft. by 28 ft.—which was probably used originally as a dining room for such a large family: ten children plus the parents and the many guests who apparently frequented Ayr Mount. Mr. Kirkland's inventory at his death in 1836 lists twenty-four Windsor chairs, which may give some idea of the entertainment that took place in Ayr Mount's early days. The smaller room in the central block is something of an enigma. It might have been used as a warming room since it adjoins the dining room (the original kitchen was detached) or it could have been an office or even a guest room for the frequent visitors to Ayr Mount.

On the second floor of the central block is another large transverse hall across the north front, giving access to two commodious bedrooms on the south side of the house. There are attic rooms above the two flanking wings, originally smaller bedrooms for children. These have now been turned into bathrooms adjoining the two principal bedrooms. The stairway continues to the attic or third floor of the central block, providing one very large room—probably a bedroom, but large enough for a small dance—and a second, smaller bedroom.

The larger of the two rooms has its original paint finish from 1816; now a pale, if flaky, blue. With so many family members living at Ayr Mount, all of this space would have been needed for sleeping accommodations.

Throughout the interior of the house is the most extraordinary woodwork, which to me is the great charm of Ayr Mount, especially the handsome fireplace mantels in each room. John Sanders, in his article in *ANTIQUES*, comments that "The Georgian woodwork is somewhat heavy and old-fashioned compared to the Federal character of the house and is quite unlike the delicately scaled…woodwork and molded plaster and composition work being installed about the same time in the finest houses of eastern North Carolina." Also unusual is the four-foot-high wainscoting throughout the house, with a black baseboard at the bottom (presumably simulating marble) and topped by a boldly projecting chair rail painted a rich dark brown color throughout the house. The effect is quite striking, emphasizing the bold character of the woodwork. Also unusual is a Gothic-style cornice in the east wing or drawing room and in the large center room. The total concoction continues to defy classification by my architectural historian friends, although all concede it is pleasing. My guess is that some of the designs for the woodwork may trace to what William Kirkland himself saw and liked on his extended visit to England and Scotland shortly before he began construction. While we don't know the designer of the house, the beautiful carpentry work is known to have been executed by John J. Briggs of Raleigh, who was an ancestor of Jim Briggs, one of my closest friends when I was growing up in Raleigh.

Paint analysis by George Fore of Raleigh revealed all the original colors of Ayr Mount—including white

paint on all exterior shutters, which had later been painted black green. The original interior colors have been reapplied in all rooms except for the attic room, which retains its original paint. The plaster walls above the chair rail throughout the house were always white. The woodwork in most rooms was painted in shades of blue and green. The drawing room, or music room, had creamy white woodwork which, together with the white plaster above the chair rail, creates an elegant all-white room, enhanced by tall windows on three sides and a crystal chandelier of the period (which I added). The Kirklands' original Broadwood fortepiano, numbered and dated, sits in this room as it always has.

While paint analysis determined the color schemes, David Byers and Browne & Company in Atlanta created simple yet elegant hangings, suitable for a house of this period and quality, for the windows in all rooms. Venetian shades, painted green, were used frequently in early-nineteenth-century North Carolina to shutter the light, and are used at all the windows in lieu of under curtains. Throughout the house we have mixed the Kirklands' original furnishings, to the extent I have been able to locate their things, with my own collection of Federal-period Duncan Phyfe antiques, mostly dated 1810-15—the exact period of Ayr Mount's construction. It seems to me that this Federal furniture looks much better and more at home in Ayr Mount than in my other houses, which were built in a later, neo-classical period.

The entrance transverse hall of Ayr Mount is covered with a floor cloth in a brown and beige octagon pattern painted recently by John Kraus. This treatment, simulating marble, was frequently used during the early nineteenth century.

The upright, straight-backed Phyfe sofas and chairs seem right at home in Ayr Mount. With a fire in the fireplace on a chilly afternoon, someone (not me) playing the Kirklands' old Broadwood fortepiano (it has been fully restored), with tea or something stronger served, and candlelight, there is no more gracious and civilized setting for polite conversation. In fact, the conversation almost *has* to be polite in such a setting!

As in the case of my other houses, I have been amazed by how many original Kirkland possessions have returned to Ayr Mount. One such item was a long-sought portrait of Judge William Gaston, the father of Susan Gaston Donaldson of Edgewater, which I had been seeking. While visiting one of the Kirkland relatives—May Reynolds, in South Carolina—I was stunned to see the portrait of Judge Gaston on the wall. I later learned that a grandson of William Kirkland had married a granddaughter of Judge Gaston. I was able to acquire the Gaston portrait, and it now hangs at Ayr Mount. But the portrait would be equally at home at Edgewater, since Robert Donaldson's estate inventory listed a portrait of Judge Gaston, which was why I had been seeking it. Small world!

Because of the historical importance of Ayr Mount and the role of the Kirkland family, and other North Carolina families connected to the Kirklands by marriage, I commissioned Jean Bradley Anderson, a respected North Carolina historian, to write a history of the house and the Kirkland Family. The result was her book, *The Kirklands of Ayr Mount* (University of North Carolina Press, 1991), which has become the definitive work on Ayr Mount. John Sanders' article in the May 1989 issue of *ANTIQUES* also is an excellent resource on Ayr Mount's history.

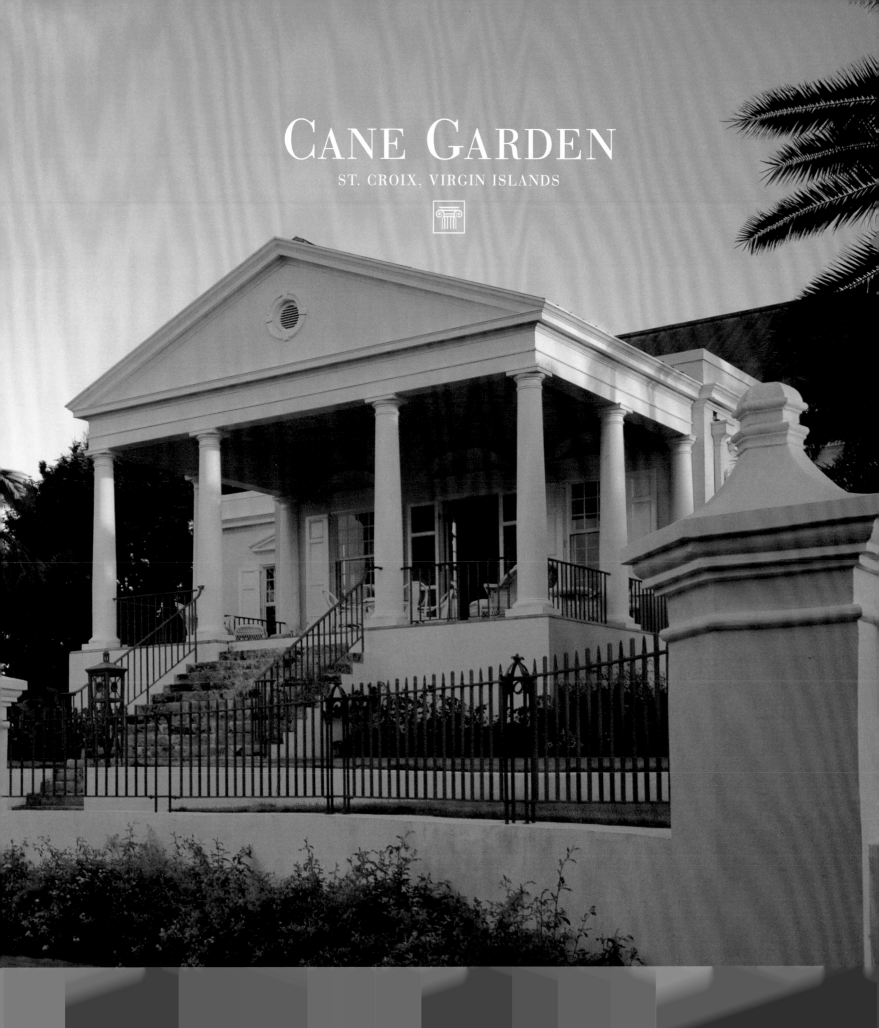

CANE GARDEN

ST. CROIX, VIRGIN ISLANDS

CHAPTER 11

CANE GARDEN

When I am back in New York thinking that I should simplify my life by not owning so many houses, I ask myself, "Do I really need a house in the Virgin Islands?" It's so far away and I really don't use it that much. Each fall there are hurricanes to worry about. But when cold weather comes and I return to Cane Garden, an old St. Croix sugar cane plantation located on a high hill overlooking the blue Caribbean, I always conclude it would be the height of folly not to keep such an extraordinary house in such a choice location. In addition to its splendid late-eighteenth-century "Great House," Estate Cane Garden today still includes some 200 acres of land and a mile of beautiful beach. It's probably a lot better investment than Treasury bonds, which is probably what I would do with the money if I sold it, and certainly a lot more fun than clipping coupons.

(Preceding) The original elliptically shaped Danish walls are an integral part of the classical architecture of Cane Garden. (Left) Life is sweet in this idyllic tropical setting, sheltered from sun and rain by eight Doric columns on a high hill overlooking the Caribbean Sea.

The feeling of the place is not unlike Monticello, Thomas Jefferson's beloved mountaintop home in Virginia. I'm sure Mr. Jefferson would have loved this little villa with even prettier views.

Indeed, in many ways Cane Garden is the most livable of all my six houses. Granted, the summers are long and hot—though Cane Garden, on its high hill by the sea, is cooled year-around by trade winds. The winter months are absolutely delightful; *delicious* is the right word. Day after day of blue skies, gentle breezes, mild temperature, flowers everywhere, swimming in the blue Caribbean and, to nurture the soul of an architectural buff like me, an exquisite small late-eighteenth-century Palladian villa—just the right size not to overwhelm, but large enough for entertaining. The feeling of the place is not unlike Monticello, Thomas Jefferson's beloved mountaintop home in Virginia. I'm sure Mr. Jefferson would have loved this little villa with even prettier views. To the south, east and west one sees (and hears) the blue Caribbean, changing from one breathtaking shade of blue to another as the sun moves across the horizon. On the land side, the house overlooks a valley of green fields, once planted as far as the eye could see in sugar cane (hence the name Cane Garden).

To ascend my little mountain, one passes through a pair of the plantation's original tall Danish gates and follows a long winding driveway lined with ancient

Miles of nearly empty beaches stretch eastward from Estate Cane Garden. The incredibly blue water constantly changes its hue with the movement of sun and clouds.

The south side of Cane Garden overlooks the Caribbean Sea. The high hipped roof and "welcoming arms" staircase are characteristic features of St. Croix's Danish colonial architecture.

tamarind trees, at least 200 years old. Not until one reaches the top of the hill is the house visible, coming as something of a surprise since the Doric columns and architectural details on the façade are somewhat grander than is found elsewhere on the island.

Mercifully, the area around Cane Garden has minimal development, to the chagrin of local developers. My 200 acres are dwarfed by thousands of acres owned by my neighbors—Walls, Nelthropps, Gasperis— and, so far, kept in a natural state. In the eyes of most

*Busts of Thomas Jefferson and George Washington,
my patron saints, watch over the classical architecture
of the Great Hall, with its 24-foot high tray ceiling.
A profusion of bougainvillea on the grounds makes
flower arranging easy, even for me.*

people the only blemish in this earthly paradise is a huge refinery, one of the world's largest, a few miles to the west. It's far enough away so that I neither see, hear, nor smell it. I've planted a forest that screens out the view, just as the trade winds blow noise and smells from the refinery in the opposite direction from my house. I must say, however, that even a refinery can be beautiful at night. From the other side of my "green screen" the view of the refinery from my mountaintop looks like some vast city spreading into

the distance at night. People pay a fortune for views of the lights of Los Angeles from nearby hills, and here I'm blocking it out!

The net effect is to feel that Cane Garden is way out in the country, and in many ways it is. The only sound is the sea roaring in the distance. The nearest town, Christiansted, is over the mountains to the north, six or seven miles away, which is close enough to access restaurants and enjoy the handsome (though sadly

A colorful red Turkish carpet that was de-accessioned years ago by Boscobel in New York State has found its way to St. Croix as a centerpiece of the Great Hall. The large over-stuffed sofa and chairs also have a history—they once belonged to Mrs. Robert R. Young, widow of the railroad magnate and sister of Georgia O'Keeffe, in her Palm Beach home.

The handsome pair of large gilt mirrors also came from Boscobel. The set of twenty drawings of St. Petersburg in 1820 served as an architectural guide for me on a recent trip to Russia. Most of the classical buildings shown in this suite of prints are still in existence. The old Island mahogany desk and most of the other furnishings in the room were made in the Caribbean in the early nineteenth century.

disappearing) Danish eighteenth- and early-nineteenth-century architecture that still prevails there.

Indeed, one feels the presence of the Danes throughout the Island and especially so at Cane Garden. Prior to my occupancy, the queen of Denmark visited Cane Garden during the occupancy of the Wall family, which preceded me. Also, I get regular requests for tours from groups in Copenhagen seeking a return to Denmark's age of empire. Built in 1784 and probably

The dining room features more Island mahogany furniture and a blue carpet of classical motifs, designed by Bill Thompson and made by Scalamandré. The silver 1820 English crystal chandelier from Nesle has survived several hurricanes. The large American convex mirror and sideboard were in the dining room when I bought the house. Flowers by my housekeeper, Cynthia Armantrading.

enlarged and remodeled along classical lines in 1820, Cane Garden was owned by the McEvoy family for three generations during the eighteenth and nineteenth centuries. Scotch-Irish by ancestry, the McEvoys converted to Danish citizenship and became successful planters in the Danish West Indies. Said to have been fabulously rich off sugar cane, the senior McEvoy, who

Tucked below the main floor of Cane Garden is a full floor of guest bedrooms. Windows are at ground level. This guest room has its own doorway to a private courtyard with a view to the ocean.

(Right) An upstairs bedroom features one of many old Island mahogany four-poster beds throughout the house. Originally the beds would have been hung with a gauze-like mosquito netting.

also owned three castles in Denmark, once aroused the king's ire by appearing (in Copenhagen) in a coach drawn by eight white horses—a distinction evidently reserved for the king. McEvoy was later forgiven and continued to produce enormous wealth for the Danes (Denmark owned St. Croix until World War I, when it was sold to the U.S.). The McEvoy family also owned Whim, another South Shore sugar cane plantation, ten miles west of Cane Garden. The original sugar mills

of both Cane Garden and Whim are still standing near the houses. Whim Great House is now open to the public for tours. Its unusual elliptical shape (surrounded by a moat) makes it well worth a visit and is indicative of the McEvoy family's sophistication in architecture.

I also learned that in the seventeenth century, when St. Croix was under French control, the property now called Cane Garden was owned by a Count DuVal. Since my mother had DuVal French ancestry on one side of her family, that added a bit of personal interest to my ownership. DuVal eventually turned the property over to a Jesuit monastery. Architectural historians believe part of today's Cane Garden Great House was originally the old monastery. The two-and-one-half-foot-thick walls suggest it was built for the ages. Certainly the site high on a hill with such a view over the Caribbean would have been a perfect place for monastic contemplation.

The house today is not exactly the original, but is as close as I could make it. A disastrous fire at the beginning of the twentieth century destroyed the roof, flooring, and all interior woodwork, leaving only the shell of massive stone walls, porches, staircases and columns as a ghostly monument to its former grandeur. The house stood as a romantic ruin for the next fifty years, gradually overrun by weeds and vines, until it was rescued and rebuilt following the end of World War II by the Howard Wall family of Portland, Oregon. Prior to their rebuilding, the Walls had detailed, close-up photographs taken of the ruins from all angles, as a record for posterity. These photographs were crucial to my later restoration efforts. The Walls proceeded to rebuild the interior to their own specifications, incorporating all of the thick standing walls but deleting the original distinctive high hipped roof in favor of a lower, probably more hurricane resistant,

CANE GARDEN
Floor Plan

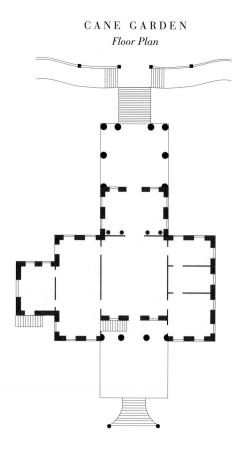

solid cement ceiling and low roof. The house would have made a good bomb shelter, something I needed when Hurricane Hugo roared through with 200 mph winds a couple of years after I finished my restoration.

When I bought Cane Garden in 1985, I could have moved right in and done nothing to the house and been a lot richer. It was strongly built and handsome in its way, but not the original look. Being addicted to classical architecture, I could not resist the impulse to try to return Cane Garden to its original state, particularly since I had the "footprints" of the original in dozens of photographs of the burned-out ruins, which showed all the original walls, locations of interior doors, windows, columns, etc. In rebuilding the house, Mr. & Mrs. Wall had saved a yard full of stone fragments from the

original house—broken columns, pieces of the stone cornice around the roof, etc.—all revealing the elegant character of the original house. Moreover, I had been introduced to Fred Gjessing, a highly regarded Danish architect residing in St. Thomas and the resident authority on early Danish colonial architecture. Having just sold DLJ to The Equitable, with money to spend (always a dangerous period in one's life), I decided to go the "full Monty"—returning Cane Garden to its original state, as nearly as our sleuthing could ascertain.

With another local architect, William Taylor of St. Croix, assisting Gjessing, we embarked on what turned out to be a fascinating, if expensive, three-year research and rebuilding process. We searched ancient archives in Copenhagen and sought recollections from the Nelthropp family, which had owned Cane Garden when it burned. One particularly helpful find was a proposed architectural drawing by architect Herbert Nelthropp (now deceased) for rebuilding Cane Garden along the original lines, including the high, hipped roof so characteristic of Island architecture. These plans were abandoned by the Walls in favor of a much lower roof and a simplified façade.

While the rebuilding process that I subsequently undertook was long and expensive, since it involved undoing some of what the Walls had done as well as rebuilding according to Fred Gjessing's new designs, I have long since concluded it was worth it. The house today is eminently satisfactory to me, not only visually but as a comfortable place to live and entertain.

The original structure of Cane Garden, perhaps from its monastery days, was a long rectangle with the interior divided into three large rooms separated by thirty-inch-thick walls. The huge center room, the largest of the three, would have been used for receptions during the house's years as the plantation's Great House. The twenty-four-foot-high tray ceiling, going up into the roof of the house, creates a cool, airy space. The eastern third of the rectangle, which gets the best breezes, was probably one huge master or communal bedroom (now divided into two bedrooms). The western third of the rectangle is now and probably always was a large dining room stretching from north to south, overlooking the sea. The original kitchen—still existing as a "romantic ruin"—was detached, with food brought up steps to a serving porch (now my kitchen) just off the dining room.

Cane Garden appears to have been remodeled in the then fashionable neo-classical style around 1820, when Christopher McEvoy, Jr., transferred ownership to his nephew, Peter McEvoy. It has been suggested that the architect both for the original house and later remodeling may have been Dr. William Thornton, one of the architects who worked on the Capitol in Washington, D.C. Dr. Thornton, a prominent amateur architect and friend of Thomas Jefferson, was born in the Virgin Islands and returned there in 1786, about the time Cane Garden was built. He probably would have known the prominent McEvoy family. In any event, Cane Garden looks very much like a miniature version of the White House. The alternating triangular and demi-lune pediments (or "eyebrows") over all of the tall windows are very similar to those at the White House.

The principal thrust of the circa 1820 remodeling was to add a new Grecian temple-form wing extending to the north, terminating with a colonnade of Doric columns. The new wing created a T-cross effect with the old rectangular main block of the house. This addition includes a second reception room (perhaps for the ladies) separated from the larger central reception room of the old house by an interior screen of Doric columns, allowing breezes to blow through, but assuring a certain privacy in each reception area. The north end of this new wing terminates in a very spacious and delightful covered porch—surrounded by four Doric columns on the front (supporting a classical triangular pediment and roof) and two more columns on either side. This porch, filled with comfortable wicker furniture, seems to be everyone's favorite seating area. Completing this architectural *tour de force* is a truly grand staircase (suitable for the Grand March from *Aida*), descending from the porch to what would have been (and still are) the owner's pleasure gardens.

Thus Dr. Thornton, or some clever architect, took what was essentially a typical rectangular Island house, without many distinguishing features, and turned it into a neo-classical jewel, with the handsome colonnaded porch on the north, or land, side overlooking the valley below. When St. Croix was primarily agricultural, the columns of the house would have been visible miles away, looming over the vast fields of sugar cane like some ancient Grecian temple.

Balancing this colonnaded north porch is an uncovered large stone terrace of similar scale on the south, or ocean, side of Cane Garden. This is the single best place for viewing the Caribbean, especially in late afternoon as the water turns a vivid blue, with whitecaps rolling in to shore at the foot of the hill. This blue contrasts with a velvet green lawn and a hedge of crimson bougainvillea rambling over a low stone wall defining the lawn on all sides. The terrace has its original "welcoming arms" staircase, a typical feature of Danish architecture, leading to the lawn on the seaside.

The effect of all this is to create a "parade of rooms," much prized in the eighteenth and nineteenth centuries. Arrival by visitors was probably from the ocean side, as it usually is today, and the visitor would have ascended to the south terrace via the "welcoming arms" staircase. This would provide the *first experience* for visitors to Cane Garden: a stunning 180-degree panoramic view of the Caribbean. From the terrace one enters the Great Hall, with its dramatic twenty-four-foot-high tray ceiling, providing the *second experience*. The eye then sees through the screen of interior Doric columns on the far side of the Great Hall, inviting the visitor to proceed to the second reception room in the north wing, creating the *third experience*. Continuing on the same axis, one then moves to the *fourth experience*: the spacious north porch, surrounded by columns on all sides with a view of the valley and mountains to the north and side views back to the sea. The *fifth experience* is down the long staircase from the porch to the pleasure gardens, which are shielded from the prevailing trade winds that make horticulture difficult at the seaside.

The elliptically shaped pleasure gardens are on level ground. The ellipse is defined by original high protective walls on the side toward the mansion—presumably for

The centerpiece of my bedroom furniture is a late-eighteenth-century four-poster Newport, R.I. bed, found in St. Croix. It faces windows to the south overlooking the blue Caribbean—not a bad way to wake up every morning. Throughout the house, all windows are equipped with both interior shutters to control light and wind and exterior shutters which we close each fall when hurricane season approaches.

security reasons, with the ever-present danger of slave insurrections in the early nineteenth century. There is a walkway along the top of the walls that looks like it might have been designed for use by a sentry or guard during periods of unrest, which evidently were frequent. The far north side of the elliptical garden is defined by what looks like a low wall from within the garden, but is actually another high stone wall, when viewed from the other side. This wall serves as a retaining wall to support the level garden surface which otherwise would have been a downward sloping hillside. It also would have provided a second, or outer, perimeter of defense in case of trouble. In many ways, the walls around Cane Garden conjure up the image of a fortress on a mountaintop, yet the place manages to remain friendly and welcoming.

It's easy for me to imagine elegant receptions given by the McEvoys in this pleasure garden, with the classical columns of the villa looming impressively above. The elliptically curved garden walls, interspersed by six high square pillars with pyramidal caps, become an integral part of the architecture of the house. This creates the illusion of a widely spread villa, which reminds me of the villas of Palladio in northern Italy that string out stables and barns on either side of the main residence to make it seem more impressive.

Actually, Cane Garden is a good deal bigger than it looks from the exterior. While the house gives the impression of being only a one-story house, with the single floor built on a basement platform, there is in fact a full floor of bedrooms below the *piano nobile*. Originally, the center of this ground level floor was a giant cistern for gathering and holding water. There were small service rooms, presumably for servants or storage, around the sides (or possibly dormitory rooms when the

house was a monastery). Somewhere along the way, the basement ceiling was raised, taking a foot or two off the main floor above but adding enough height to create five comfortable guest bedrooms and a central hall (where the cistern used to be) on the ground floor.

Thus, Cane Garden achieves the fashionable early-nineteenth-century look of a single-story, classical Greek or Roman temple, with another floor hidden away on the basement level. At Jefferson's Monticello the reverse was

The doorway on the south side of the Great Hall provides a spectacular view down the hillside to the Caribbean Sea. The red silk fringe curtains were made by Anthony Hail some 30 years ago for Edgewater, but have migrated to St. Croix and still manage to look stylish.

the case; the second floor with lower ceilings was hidden away above the *piano nobile*. I prefer the arrangement at Cane Garden, where guests or children have their own private rooms on a separate floor with several ground level entrances opening directly to the gardens. Two of the ground floor bedrooms open into their own private walled gardens. Guests can come and go as they wish. There is no interior staircase between the two floors, enhancing security on the main floor. Instead, there is an outside stone staircase descending from the terrace on the ocean side of the house to the ground floor. This staircase had been cemented over at some time in the past to enlarge the terrace, probably by the Walls who cut an inside stairway (since closed by me) at the back end of the dining room. We found the old staircase, still intact, almost by accident while rebuilding Cane Garden. With this discovery I was able to eliminate the interior staircase which I felt destroyed the symmetry (to say nothing of the privacy) of the dining room.

As a result of these features, the principal floor, or *piano nobile* can remain blissfully peaceful even though there may be a full floor of people coming and going to the five bedrooms below. There are also two bedrooms on the *piano nobile*, so if there are no guests the basement floor can be simply shut off. While the main floor is very commodious and airy, it is also very compact, with all the amenities—kitchen, dining room, bed and bath, as well as the grand parlors and two porches—all on the same level. In old age, one could be very content to live just on the main floor of Cane Garden, admiring the classical architecture and the constantly changing view out to sea or over the valley.

The overall feeling of Cane Garden could be described in two words: *light* and *airy*. Most of the rooms are painted white, and there are windows everywhere, each lined up with interior doorways to permit a free flow of breeze in the tropical climate. For hurricanes, there are exterior shutters and interior shutters, the latter also used to shield out light that gets too bright at times. The shutters and roof, built in the old Island manner with ample ventilation, came through the acid test of Hurricane Hugo with flying colors. Cane Garden was the only house in the neighborhood with its roof still intact after Hugo passed by.

I should mention one other feature that adds to the pleasure and ambiance of a visit to Cane Garden—the unique Island antique mahogany furniture scattered throughout the house. This includes giant four-poster beds, chairs, sofas, and sideboards, all made in the Caribbean of local mahogany some 150-175 years ago. And surprise: I didn't collect it, despite my penchant for antique furniture. The bulk of it was collected by Mrs. Howard Wall, who loved old Island-made mahogany furniture and began to collect it shortly after WWII when *nobody* wanted antique furniture, especially the slightly naive Island-made furniture. Most of the furniture was made in the early nineteenth century and has a handsome English Regency look about it. I was able to buy most of Mrs. Wall's interesting collection at the time I bought the house. None of it is original to Cane Garden, but all of it was made in the local area. Since my restoration of Cane Garden, I have continued to add to the collection. In recent years, Island mahogany antique furniture has once again become fashionable and highly prized. I'm sure Mrs. Wall would not have been surprised. Incidentally, if there are spirits lingering on, I am sure it is Mrs. Wall; she truly loved Cane Garden, as do I.

THE GEORGE F. BAKER HOUSE

NEW YORK CITY

CHAPTER 12

THE GEORGE F. BAKER HOUSE

PART I

Even before I saw the house I was predisposed to it. George Fisher Baker (1842-1932) had been one of my larger-than-life heroes in business history.

Finding a great place to live in Manhattan is a little like looking for the Holy Grail. Unlike London or Paris with their huge stock of fine residential properties, the supply of first-class town houses in New York City is surprisingly limited, given the wealth and large population of the city. Most wealthy New Yorkers, perhaps for security reasons, prefer to live in cooperative apartments, just as I did when I bought my first "co-op" at 455 East 57th Street. But I am far too independent to put up with the constraints of apartment house living, even in a prestigious Park Avenue or Fifth Avenue address.

And so like Diogenes with his lantern, I have searched for nearly forty years to find the perfect house in which to live in Manhattan. I came close a number of times: One Sutton Place North (couldn't afford it);

(Preceding) No. 67 East 93rd Street was built as a residence for George F. Baker at age 90. The arched doorway on the right (69 East 93rd Street) led to the Bakers' carriage house.
(Left) A side view of 69 East 93rd Street with its paired Ionic columns.

37 Charlton Street (inconvenient location); 150 East 38th Street (too small); 27 East 11th Street (rent control tenants). Before I bought my co-op at 455 East 57th Street, I also had lived in at least a half dozen rental apartments. So I have lived, as the song goes, "East Side, West Side, all around the town." The only place I never lived that *seemed* attractive (if you work in nearby Wall Street) was Brooklyn Heights, filled with interesting early-nineteenth-century town houses, some with breathtaking views of Manhattan and the harbor.

As I have noted before, houses have a way of finding me, especially when you are a friend of Edward Lee Cave, Manhattan's most renowned realtor of fine residential properties. After I had moved my offices from the Wall Street area to The Equitable uptown, the house I owned at 37 Charlton Street was no longer so convenient. I also was a bit tired of the downtown location, and had begun to think of a move back to the Upper East Side, where I had begun my life in New York City. I had more or less gotten over my bohemian, "Village" period. Thus, I was in a receptive mood when Edward Lee Cave called my attention to the George F. Baker House at 67 East 93rd Street.

A long marble hallway connects the yellow reception room at the front of the house and the oval dining room in the rear, bypassing the stairwell in between.

(Right) Cheerful yellow walls, architectural drawings, and a fire in the fireplace of the reception room provide a warm welcome to the house. The French early-nineteenth-century wallpaper is by Dufour.

Even before I saw the house I was predisposed to it. George Fisher Baker (1842-1932) had been one of my larger-than-life heroes in business history. I first heard of the legendary Mr. Baker when I was admitted to the Harvard Business School back in 1955. The letterhead of my acceptance letter read "Harvard University Graduate School of Business Administration, George F. Baker Foundation." I later learned that Mr. Baker, a long-time head and principal stockholder of the old First National Bank of New York (which later became First National City Bank, finally shortened in name but not size to today's global colossus Citibank), had given *all* the money (he specified he wanted to do it all alone) to build the Harvard Business School's spectacular Georgian campus lying along the banks of the Charles River. So, even before seeing the house, I liked the idea of owning George F. Baker's house in New York City.

In fact, No. 67 East 93rd Street turned out to be a very handsome brick Georgian-style town house which perfectly suited my traditional tastes in architecture. It even looked like the Harvard Business School! The architects had been Delano & Aldrich, who, along with McKim, Mead & White, were responsible for much of New York's greatest architecture in the early twentieth century. The house also bore many similarities to my long-lost One Sutton Place, "the one that got away."

No. 67 East 93rd Street had been built for Mr. Baker very late in his life (he died in 1932, at age ninety, and the house was not completed until that same year). There is some debate as to whether he actually got to live in his new house before his death. Mr. Baker's son, George F. Baker, Jr., owned the large Georgian town house next door on the corner of 93rd Street and Park Avenue (now owned by the Russian Orthodox Church).

Evidently George Jr. wanted the aging patriarch of the family to live close by (Mrs. Baker, Senior, had died some years earlier). And so the Bakers commissioned Delano & Aldrich to design a town house suitable for an elderly gentleman—Mr. Baker (but I'm getting there!).

The house is literally a fortress: everything is built double thick and fireproof. It could be a bomb shelter if the need arose. Interior stairways for servants also serve as fire escapes, with slate floors, iron railings, nothing flammable. So solidly is the house built that there is not a creak or groan to be heard in the house nor cracks to be found anywhere, even after nearly seventy years of occupancy. Most of the original appliances still work: furnace, elevator, sink, tubs, etc. The Bakers built for the ages!

Like One Sutton Place North, 67 East 93rd Street is only one room wide (twenty feet) across the front. The windows, in the English Regency style, are very tall, extending all the way to the floor. The ceilings at twelve feet are above average in height for a Manhattan town house (higher than One Sutton, I was pleased to note). The length of the house is seventy feet, extending almost to the back of the property line. In this respect, the house is very reminiscent of One Sutton Place—long and narrow with a similar very grand circular staircase ascending through the center of the house. Large rooms open off either side of the stairwell hall on all three of the principal floors. If anything, the staircase is even more elegant than One Sutton Place because the ceilings are higher and there is a handsome round skylight at the top which gives the feeling of a rotunda.

To make a long story short, the house suited me perfectly. The price, $4 million, was *far* more than I had ever paid for a house (nearly ten times what I had paid

I have moved this same antique French wallpaper by Dufour three times, no doubt contributing to its antiquity. It's titled Fêtes de la Grèce et Jeux Olympiques.

(Left) The stairwell at Baker House is reminiscent of One Sutton Place North, including the ornamental hall lantern which reappears here.

for One Sutton Place, the previous highest price I had paid for a house in New York). I was able to sell my existing residence (the Federal-period town house at 37 Charlton Street) for $2 million—a large gain over my $250,000 purchase price —which eased the pain of this new purchase. This gain also eased some of the pain of having sold One Sutton Place so cheaply, since part of those proceeds had gone to buy 37 Charlton Street.

Within a week after I had bought 67 East 93rd Street and sold 37 Charlton Street, the stock market suddenly collapsed on October 19, 1987. This was the frightening

Tiring of no-color walls, I found this rich blue color in a book about the Petits Appartements *of Marie Antoinette at Versailles. The resemblance stops with the color.*

(Left) The drawing room mantel is flanked by a pair of tall French Charles X bookcases, circa 1820. A pair of French bouillotte lamps, made and signed by Pierre-Philippe Thomire, and a gilt English convex mirror brighten the room.

508 point, 23% drop in the market, the most precipitous one-day decline since the Depression 1930s. Because my new house bore such a resemblance to One Sutton Place, I thought to myself "My God, I've done it again: overspent on a big town house just as hard times come."

I began to feel that houses built in the late 1920s must bring me bad luck! Karen Bechtel, a high-

powered Morgan Stanley investment banker who had paid the $2 million for my house at 37 Charlton Street, wasn't too happy either. I tried to console her by pointing out that I had laid out twice that amount for 67 East 93rd Street, on the theory that "misery loves company" and that I really had no inkling the stock market was about to collapse when I sold her my house. Happily, the market sell-off was short-lived this time (unlike 1974 which was followed by nearly a *decade* of bad markets). Karen Bechtel still owns 37 Charlton Street and loves it. The house seemed to bring her luck, as it did me. Her Morgan Stanley stock has gone up and up since then.

I was perhaps battle scarred from my 1974 experience at One Sutton Place and, so, only a little more than a year later I said "yes" when an acquaintance called me (just as Drue Heinz had done on One Sutton Place) and offered what seemed to me a very high price—$6 million—for 67 East 93rd Street. I decided to let it go and pocket a quick $2 million gain.

Instead of having to retreat once again to an apartment, as I did after selling One Sutton Place, fate dealt me a better hand this time (Ed Cave to the rescue!). Next door to 67 East 93rd Street was an elegant brick structure (69 East 93rd Street) that had served as the Bakers' carriage house when the family owned practically the entire neighborhood. This carriage house, which did not look *at all* like a carriage house,

Another view of the Blue Drawing Room. The Adam-style English pier mirror, which once hung in the hall of One Sutton Place, seems right at home between the two tall windows. The chandelier is English, circa 1800.

impressed me with its ornamental colonnade of four matched pairs of tall Ionic columns along one side, sheltering a narrow porch overlooking a large courtyard that had belonged to George F. Baker, Jr. (when he owned the house on the corner of Park and 93rd Street). The carriage house, which also housed servant quarters, had been turned into a single-family apartment in recent years by George F. Baker IV, who lived there with his wife and family. The younger Baker had decided to move and sell, just at the time I sold No. 67 next door.

And so I bought it for $4 million, which seemed like a lot considering the fact that most of the first floor was a gigantic six-car garage, and the upstairs area

Everyone's favorite room at 67 East 93rd Street seems to be the elegant oval dining room, which takes its glory from the beautiful hand-cut marble flooring installed by the Bakers in the late 1920s when the house was built. The dark chocolate walls pick up the brown and beige colors of the marble.

was rather cut up into small rooms. But the *exterior* of 69 East 93rd Street was absolutely fabulous—one of the most handsome facades in Manhattan. Because it overlooked the courtyard, there was light on all sides (if one includes an interior "light court" between No. 67

and No. 69). The tall Ionic columns, built one floor above street level for added height (like my house in Charleston), were really intended for show rather than function; an elegant backdrop to the Baker's so-called "French courtyard," which once sported a fountain. I felt that with such a handsome exterior envelope (also by Delano & Aldrich) I could eventually reconfigure the inside into a more stylish arrangement of rooms for living and entertaining. Finally, with my $2 million windfall gain on the sale of No. 69, I reasoned that I would have a net of only $2 million invested in this residence (and if I had included the earlier nearly $2 million gain on the sale of 37 Charlton Street, I would be living in a fine house in Manhattan with virtually nothing invested, just like Gus Levy bragged to me about the co-op apartment he bought during the Depression). A final benefit was that I felt I was not being completely disloyal to the memory of my hero, George F. Baker, since his family had also owned this building.

For the next seven years (1989 to 1996) I lived quite happily at No. 69 East 93rd Street in what had been the Baker's carriage house. I liked the light and the height of the ceilings, but the house lacked a grand ceremonial entrance staircase as I had enjoyed next door at 67 East 93rd Street and before that at One Sutton Place. I even went so far as to commission Michael Dwyer, my favorite young neo-classical architect in Manhattan, to design a new interior layout. His plan "borrowed" half the six-car garage on the first floor and

A portrait of Daniel Tompkins, Governor of New York and Vice President under James Monroe, dated 1819 by Charles Willson Peale, gazes benignly over the oval dining room.

would have created an elegant entrance hall and elliptical staircase ascending to the *piano nobile* (as well as an elevator tucked in the back).

But before I could implement Mike Dwyer's plans, fate intervened again. The individual who had bought 67 East 93rd Street from me decided that he wanted to sell. He was willing to accept a substantial discount from the $6 million he had paid me in order to sell quickly. The price this time was $5 million—a $1 million discount from the price at which I had sold it seven years previous. It seemed a fair price at the time, though town house prices had risen again in the wake of Wall Street prosperity, the inevitable lubricant for raising Manhattan real estate prices.

I decided to move back into No. 67, which was more a "proper" house (as someone said) than was the carriage house. That left the problem of what to do with No. 69 East 93rd Street. Edward Lee Cave said that the two properties, side by side, would be more valuable kept together. Nor did I really want to sell No. 69, whose elegant multi-columned side façade was, to my way of thinking, the most handsome domestic architecture in New York. Who else in Manhattan has eight Ionic columns on their house? And so I decided to keep both properties.

More recently, I have concluded that No. 69 (the carriage house) would make an ideal headquarters for all my preservation activities, which stretch from New York to the Caribbean. The foundation I established, Classical American Homes Preservation Trust, will eventually own all, or most, of my houses—to be operated as house museums if that seems feasible.

The bottom line: I don't think Mr. Baker wants me to sell either of these houses!

CHAPTER 13

THE GEORGE F. BAKER HOUSE

PART II

When I moved back into 67 East 93rd Street, the house somehow seemed different, more elegant, than when I owned it before. I became more conscious of the really extraordinary quality of workmanship in the house. For example, the entire first floor—from the front door to the central stair hall to an oval dining room in the rear of the house—is fitted out with the most exquisite marble floor I have ever seen, in two colors of marble: beige and brown. Each square was individually cut, fitting so snugly it was not even necessary to insert metal strips for a tighter fit.

The craftsmanship reaches a crescendo in the oval dining room. There is an elaborate geometric design in marble, cut in curves, complementing the sinuous curves of the oval-shaped room. The glistening marble floor, highly polished, makes you want to dance! The cost of so painstakingly cutting and intricately fitting the marble would be almost prohibitive today. While I had admired this marble floor when I owned the house before, I have to admit it looks much better now. The previous owner had the marble painstakingly cleaned

The grand spiral staircase at 67 East 93rd Street.

Having had the equivalent of a post-graduate degree from working with so many great interior designers over the years, I decided to forego an outside decorator.

by hand and polished to a high gloss. It literally "knocks your socks off."

Since I still owned No. 69 (the carriage house next door) there was no great rush to move back into No. 67. I could do things slowly and experiment. Having had the equivalent of a post-graduate degree from working with so many great interior designers over the years, I decided to forego an outside decorator (the best ones were too busy, anyway) and use my own team of artisans that I have worked with in the past. Also, I felt I had gotten somewhat in a rut with my decorating: walls were inevitably marbleized (no color, goes with everything, but getting boring for me) and the furnishings were the obligatory Federal or American Empire, all mahogany, early nineteenth century. I decided I wanted to do something different in this house.

I started in the beautiful oval dining room on the first floor, with its fabulous beige and brown marble floor. The room tended to be on the dark side (north side of the house with windows only at one end) and I decided there was no way I could make it light. Instead, I decided to go the other way and paint it a dark color—a rich chocolate brown, keying off the beige and brown marble floor. This meant using

artificial light even in the daytime, but it proved to be a great success. Everything stood out in sharp relief: the white marble mantel, white Ionic pilasters, four marble busts of British prime ministers, a gold convex mirror over the sideboard, gold frames on pictures. I also found a magnificent early-nineteenth-century French Empire ormolu chandelier at Nesle's (to my mind the world's best source of chandeliers), which pulls the room together. Jack Smith, my jack-of-all-trades, rigged up a way to light the chandelier from below, highlighting the gold-gilt base. Bill Thompson and his Barrytown Associates whipped up some yellow and white curtains with swags for the three tall windows in the rear, which complemented the brown color of the walls. With soft lights highlighting the rich brown color, the room at night becomes very warm and conversational. It's different, anyway!

While in the middle of painting the oval dining room this chocolate color, I suddenly had a feeling of *déjà vu* and recalled that I had done the same thing (i.e. paint the dining room brown) at my college fraternity house at Chapel Hill nearly fifty years ago. In my senior year, I had been quite smitten by the University's new faculty lounge, which was painted in an interesting cocoa color which I had never seen used before. I can still recall the room. There were drawings of revered professors, framed with bright red matting to show them off against the dark cocoa walls. The curtains

Nos. 67-69 East 93rd Street are separated by an interior "light court." The tall secretary is New York, late eighteenth century, with carved Prince of Wales' feathers that survived the Revolution.

(Above) My library at 67 East 93rd Street was originally intended to be the bedroom of George Fisher Baker, whose portrait (center) by Frank O. Salisbury hangs above the sofa.

(Left) A handsome early-nineteenth-century gilt convex mirror hangs above a marble English mantel, circa 1800. The bookcases on either side are Irish Georgian, late eighteenth century.

(Right) Barrytown Associates did the curtains on the three windows that form a bow front to the library. The unusual German gilt chandelier, attributed to Karl Friedrich Schinkel, has a red glass insert at its base. The bronze bust is a copy of a bust of Robert Fulton by Houdon.

were beige with red piping, as I recall. Anyhow, I was so impressed that I decided something similar would look great in the Chi Psi dining room. But how do you persuade fifty guys to paint a room some chocolate color? I didn't even try. A few of us got up at 2:00 A.M. and painted the dining room, which was quite large and had lots of windows, in a chocolate color resembling what I had seen in the faculty lounge. The windows providentially already had yellow and white curtains, which cut the brown. After we had re-hung the pictures and gilt mirror over the fireplace, the room really looked great—or so we thought. Perhaps not surprisingly, most of the brothers next morning didn't even notice anything had changed! It looked nice and no one protested (I was the house president at the time and used that as my authority).

Anyhow, nearly fifty years later I am again using the same brown color scheme that worked so successfully way back in 1950 in the Chi Psi dining room.

This little trip down memory lane reminded me of another experiment in the decorating realm which I foisted on my unsuspecting fraternity brothers. The year was 1948 or 1949 and there was a decorating rage in America to paint rooms in dark, deep colors. This probably was in reaction to the insipid pale colors—light green usually—that were *de rigueur* in American homes in the 1930s and 1940s. Every fine home in Raleigh seemed to have a pale green living room. During World War II, no one could paint, so everyone was sick of Depression era/WWII color schemes by the end of the war. Somebody got the idea of using dramatic dark colors, often spread over the woodwork as well as the walls. These dark colors certainly change the feel of a room.

(Left and above) This elegant Adam-style Philadelphia mantel, circa 1800 by Robert Wellford, was installed by me to give a touch of class to the Bakers' carriage house. The early-nineteenth-century gilt French Empire clock on the mantel is quite charming, with a lady instructing her daughter in astronomy and astrology.

I first noticed this fashion one evening while walking by the Delta Kappa Epsilon fraternity house at Chapel Hill. The Dekes were known as the "rich kids," and I could usually look to them as models of how to dress, but it seemed they had become *à la mode* in decorating. The entire first floor of the Deke house had been painted a bottle blue green color. I was immediately envious. It looked so different that I stopped and stared for a long time. Later at their parties, I discovered this dark blue green looked great at night, with just a few side lights on, or even with the chandeliers turned on full-force.

I decided Chi Psi must also have a blue-green living room—and a week later we did. Once again, most people didn't seem to care what color the room was painted (as long as they didn't have to do it), though all agreed the dark color was kind of sexy at night.

Coming on the heels of my successful chocolate dining room at 67 East 93rd Street, I figured why not go all the way in reviving the dark colors that were so fashionable in the 1950s? After all, that was "my period." So for my new living room at 67 East 93rd Street I picked out a deep royal blue color (I found it in a book about Marie Antoinette's chamber at Versailles) that was remarkably similar to the color the Dekes and Chi Psi had in their living rooms fifty years ago. When I painted my new living room in this color it was a jolt at first. But when gold mirrors, pictures with gold frames, gold fabrics on furniture, etc. were dispersed around the room the deep blue color looked fabulous! The room is dramatic but also has a calming effect.

The one casualty was my mahogany antique furniture, which tends to disappear against the dark blue walls. Conveniently, just as I was pondering what to do, I found two superb tall satinwood bookcases (French, by Jacob Freres, circa 1820). I realized the blond satinwood would look perfect against the dark blue color. These bookcases, filled with leather-bound books per the

Another "blue heaven" bedroom, this one at 67 East 93rd Street. The tall secretary, made in Schenectady in 1820 for Dr. Eliphalet Nott, has migrated here from its former location at 150 East 38th Street. Virginia Pulver made all the curtains and bed hangings throughout Baker House.

Otto Zenke formula, now anchor either side of the white marble fireplace and really help lighten the room. Gradually, I am replacing the other pieces of mahogany furniture with lighter, blonder woods. Many of these pieces will be French or English, since the lighter wood colors are more difficult (though not impossible) to come by in American early-nineteenth-century antiques, where the bulk of my collection is concentrated.

So, eclectic (in collecting) seems to be back in for me (shades of Anthony Hail), as are the dark colors of the late 1940s and early 1950s. After painting my dining room the deep chocolate color, I came across an article on my favorite British designer David Hicks' apartment at the Albany in London. David had painted his "set," the proper name for one of these Albany suites, a deep chocolate brown color, just like my new dining room. And later, in Paris, I saw a newly decorated salon painted in an even deeper blue than I have used in my drawing room in New York. So, maybe the dark colors that were all the rage fifty years ago will have another run of popularity. *Plus ca change, plus c'est la meme chose!*

What else can I say about 67 East 93rd Street without getting tedious? The front hall opens into a reception room with a small but handsome marble fireplace. This room I have painted a cheerful deep yellow copied from Tommy Bennett, a friend and realtor who has owned more houses in Charleston, South Carolina, than the law allows. Tommy always has

The color scheme of this bedroom at 67 East 93rd Street was inspired by Nancy Lancaster's decorating in England. Architectural drawings by Harold Sterner.

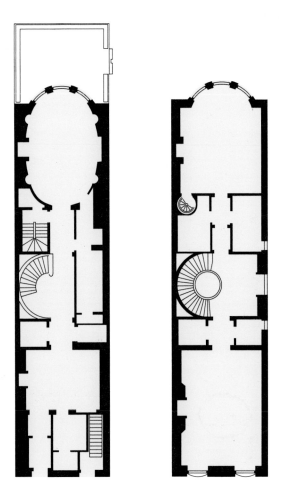

GEORGE F. BAKER HOUSE
First Floor Plan   *Third Floor Plan*

a cheerful bright yellow room in each house. This bright yellow in the hall reception room at 67 East 93rd Street is toned down by several panels of antique French wallpaper (by Dufour, circa 1815) depicting exotic Roman scenes—wild chariot rides, temples, palm trees, everything deemed exotic. The wallpaper is so old the colors have turned mostly brown, but this ties into the beige and brown marble floor. With a fire in the fireplace to warm guests on arrival, I should have a large punchbowl in the center table for further holiday cheer.

Beyond the reception room is the circular stairwell hall, which I have marbleized all the way up to the top floor—four flights above. The round stairwell, terminating in a skylight on the top floor, provides a touch of real grandeur and drama to the house. The oval chocolate dining room opens off the other side of the stairwell on the first floor, a nice complement to the yellow reception entrance hall.

The only other principal "entertaining," or public room, is the library, which was originally intended as Mr. George F. Baker's bedroom. This room is more "standard Jenrette." The carpet is a replica designed by Edward Vason Jones from an old Aubusson which I own but is now too fragile to use. I've used this carpet, featuring squares of red, beige and blue with a brown border, at DLJ and at other of my houses. It is my old reliable standby. Almost any color goes with it, and it never shows dirt or wear. The library has a handsome Georgian mantel, surmounted by the inevitable (for me) convex mirror and a French early-nineteenth-century Empire clock. There are tall bookcases, with leather-bound books, on either side of the mantel. There's a Georgian pedestal desk, another *sine qua non* for me; I think that every room should have a desk! Then there's a plaster copy of Houdon's statue of Benjamin Franklin, everybody's favorite in a library. The rest is comfortable furniture for lounging and reading.

This was probably a sitting room for George F. Baker's nurse but has been combined with a smaller room to create a large north bedroom at 67 East 93rd Street. The colorful plates on the mantel display the crest of New York's famous Livingston family.

The *pièce de résistance* of this library is a large, life-size portrait of George Fisher Baker, painted from life in 1932—the year he died and the year the house was completed. Thus, it seems totally appropriate for the room which was built as his final resting-place (for sleeping, not burial!). Mr. Baker, who was age ninety when the portrait was painted, looks at least twenty years younger.

The rest of the house is bedrooms (top floor), a mezzanine floor intended for servants (now an office), and a basement floor with an enormous kitchen (with its original dumbwaiter for the dining room above).

It is a joy to see the craftsmanship that went into this great Manhattan town house. Funny how much more I notice and appreciate the craftsmanship in this house than when I previously bought and sold it in 1987. I was so attuned to early-nineteenth-century American architecture that I perhaps failed to appreciate the great architecture and craftsmanship of the 1920s in America. Doing the decorating myself this time also may have been more satisfying. Whatever the reason, I now find this house, built for George F. Baker, to be my favorite residence of the many residences I have had in New York City over the past forty-two years.

MILLFORD PLANTATION

PINEWOOD, SOUTH CAROLINA

CHAPTER 14

MILLFORD PLANTATION:
MY TAJ MAHAL

Everybody should have a Taj Mahal of their dreams, if not in reality. For me, it has always been a white-columned house on a hill, overlooking vast fields, somewhere down south. I found my personal Taj Mahal in Millford Plantation, located in the geographic center of the state of South Carolina, rather late in life—at age sixty-three. Better late than never!

Millford is arguably the finest extant example of Greek Revival residential architecture in America. Yes, I am biased, but I've also visited most of the great examples of classical residential architecture.

Built in 1839-41 at the height of the South's pre-Civil War agricultural prosperity, Millford stands proudly on a high hill overlooking vast stretches of lawn and forest. Six gigantic stop-fluted Corinthian columns, forty feet tall, dominate the façade, supporting a massive architrave relieved only by a gently sloping pediment and punctuated by acanthus leaves at the ends and in the center. By moonlight the house almost exudes an Oriental aura, with the corners of the pediment appearing to turn up at either end as in ancient Chinese or Japanese architecture. It seems that no expense was spared in executing either the exterior or interior architectural detail.

Millford is arguably the finest extant example of Greek Revival residential architecture in America. Yes, I am biased, but I've also visited most of the great examples of classical residential architecture in America. I haven't found any of them to be its equal. The Biddles' magnificent Andalusia, outside Philadelphia, may have an even grander colonnade, but the great columns are imposed on an earlier and far less imposing house. The Custis-Lee Mansion in Arlington, Virginia has oversized columns that intimidate rather than please. It looks better from across the Potomac than up close! Berry Hill, also in Virginia and circa 1840, may make a grander spectacle at first glance with eight fluted Doric columns and matching small Greek temples on either side, but on the inside there is no comparison with Millford, which has much finer classical architectural detail. My own Roper House in Charleston, circa 1838, ranks among the best Greek Revival architecture, but Mr. Roper seems to have run low on funds in finishing the interior as his father gave away much of the family

(Preceding) The grand façade of Millford seems straight out of Gone With the Wind.
(Left) Wisteria hysteria comes to Millford in late March. The purple verbena outlining the circular loggia completes a vision of purple befitting any Roman Emperor.

fortune to build a hospital. Ashland (later called Belle Helene) on the Mississippi in Louisiana, also circa 1840, may be even more powerful and monumental than Millford, with huge square columns on all four sides, but the interiors once again are surprisingly spartan. The house was sadly a near ruin when I last saw it (the proximity to a nearby chemical plant not adding to its charms). Another one of my favorites, Gaineswood, in Demopolis, Alabama, is the opposite; it has extravagant wedding-cake-like interior plasterwork, almost to the point of suffocation, but the house itself is very unusual with columns everywhere, inside and out. It's a bit like the Roman Forum rolled into one house.

While all these houses are superb, I still give top billing to Millford as the all-around, preeminent example of American Greek Revival residential architecture. Actually, I recommend visiting *all* these previously mentioned houses if you can find a way to get in; most are open at times to the public. Each is extraordinary.

(Preceding) The back side of Millford has a different sort of grandeur—more English Regency in feel.

(Top left) The entrance hall is so wide that four Yankee horsemen were said to have ridden side by side through the hall at the end of the Civil War.

(Lower left) A stained glass oculus caps the dome of Millford's elegant circular staircase.

(Right) A view from the second floor landing to a circular trompe l'oeil painted floor by Robert Jackson.

The double parlors at Millford, separated by a screen of Corinthian columns, comprise one of America's handsomest suites of rooms. Almost all of the furnishings shown were commissioned by the Mannings from "D. Phyfe & Son," 1840-42.

Millford, the champion in my eyes, has to be seen to be believed. The visitor is probably disarmed by the remoteness of the location (ninety miles northwest of Charleston and forty-five miles southeast of Columbia, South Carolina). In driving either from Columbia or up from Charleston you don't have to pass through a single town to reach Millford. I say "up" because Millford is just outside the so-called Lowcountry that so lugubriously drapes the coastal area around Charleston in Spanish moss and cypress. One drives for nearly two hours across absolutely flat, frequently swampy country before finally encountering some hills. Then you know you are approaching Millford. This

area, called "The High Hills of Santee," must have been thrown up by some ancient volcanic eruption. In olden times it was considered more healthy than the Lowcountry, presumably because the sandy soil, which drains easily, led to fewer mosquitoes. The sandhills and longleaf pines, interspersed with moss-covered live oak, holly, magnolia and Carolina jessamine growing in wild profusion in the woods, all serve to lower visitor expectations of finding anything very civilized or architecturally grand in such a backwoods area.

But grand it is. Built foursquare with its massive and ornate Corinthian columns on the front and a Regency-like bow (enclosing a grand staircase) in the rear, Millford is imposing approached from either front or rear (or from either side for that matter). I can never decide which side I like best. The front is formal and awe-inspiring while the back, which reminds me of an English Regency villa, is actually more unusual and welcoming, with a beautiful courtyard framed by handsome dependencies in the rear. The side views convey a bit of both: restrained English Regency on the rear, and the massive columns typical of American Greek Revival on the front.

In fact, there is something neither English nor American but Germanic about the classical architecture of Millford. The house appears slightly top-heavy,

The pair of matching marble mantels were custom-made in Philadelphia for Millford, and the large gilt-frame mirrors were made in New York in 1840. All were shipped to Charleston, then up the Santee River to Millford. The furniture is documented from Phyfe's last "modern period" in the early 1840s before his death.

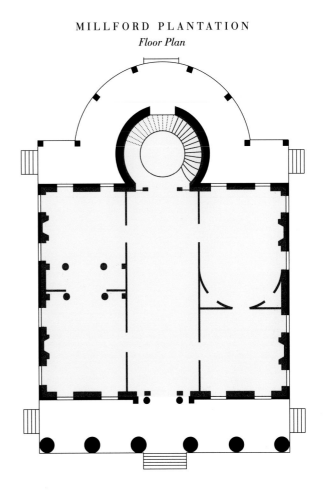

MILLFORD PLANTATION
Floor Plan

with its unusually heavy architrave surmounting the Corinthian columns. Unlike British and French architecture, where the principal floor is often elevated, Millford almost *hugs* the ground, with only a slight step up to the *piano nobile* from the ground. On either sides of the house the architrave is adorned by six acanthus leaf wreaths, concealing porthole windows in an attic floor tucked behind the massive architrave. This rather heavy, powerful look, which I find pleasing, traces to the transplanted German architect Charles Friedrich Reichardt, a pupil of Karl Friedrich Schinkel, perhaps the greatest German classical architect. Reichardt had designed the monumental Charleston Hotel, a now demolished 1830s classical hotel in Charleston. While

*The library, adjoining the dining room, shows a portrait
of Gov. John Manning temporarily resting on the floor.
Comfortable over-stuffed chairs supplant D. Phyfe & Son
in this room.*

*Almost everything in this handsome dining room, circular
at one end, is original, including the Mannings' dining
table, fourteen armchairs, two serving tables, and a wine
cellarette—all documented Duncan Phyfe.*

Millford was constructed by Nathaniel Potter, the design
he followed came straight from Reichardt's great hotel in
Charleston, which burned in 1838 and was immediately
rebuilt by Potter following the original design by
Reichardt. The overall effect achieved at Millford is
one of powerful monumentality. Years later on visiting
Berlin, I could see the same influences in Schinkel's
many surviving buildings from this period of German
classical architecture. Surviving records verify Reichardt

The spacious and comfortable dining room is the best I've ever found for long, leisurely candle-lit dinners with ample wine and amusing conversation.

(Right) The elegant classical architecture of Millford is epitomized by the door surrounds, even on the second floor of the house.

as a student at Schinkel's Bauakademie in Berlin. How he found his way to South Carolina remains something of a mystery, but he produced several notable buildings in Charleston during the city's pre-Civil War prosperity before returning eventually to Hamburg in Germany.

The mass of the central block of Millford is augmented by flanking smaller two-story wings on either side, connected by loggias supported by smaller square columns. One wing is the old kitchen (still in

The earlier, more delicate Phyfe furniture in this upstairs sitting room makes an interesting contrast to Phyfe's robust 1840-model furniture on the first floor of Millford. I shall probably return the Duncan Phyfe sofa, made in the early nineteenth century for Gov. Dewitt Clinton, back to New York.

use), the other is the original laundry (now my office). The loggias on either side extend around the back of the house, including the large cylindrical bow housing the interior staircase. Covered much of the way by ancient wisteria, which we have to keep carefully pruned lest it take over, the loggias form what Roger Kennedy, author of *Greek Revival America*, describes as a "delightful, umbrageous walk" around the entire back side of the house. I had to look up umbrageous—it means leafy and shady—but it seems to describe my back porch, or loggia, rambling around the back side of the mansion. It's a cool shady intimate area to stroll or sit on warm

days. The tall floor-to-ceiling windows opening from the main house to the loggia create a veritable decorator's showcase for viewing the handsome interiors of the house, especially when illuminated at night.

Millford was built, according to local history, by John Laurence Manning, who later became a governor of South Carolina. That's a bit of male chauvinism. In all likelihood, the house was built with *Mrs.* Manning's money. Susan Frances Hampton Manning was the daughter of Wade Hampton I, said to have been the richest man in South Carolina (if not the entire South) at the time of his death in 1838. That Susan came into a substantial portion of her father's wealth illustrates the opposite of male chauvinism—good old-fashioned *chivalry*. Wade Hampton I, as was the custom at the time, left almost his entire estate to his only son, Wade Hampton II. According to local lore, as the family gathered for the reading of the will, Wade Hampton II chivalrously tore it up and announced to all present that the estate would be shared equally with his two sisters, one of whom was Susan Frances Hampton, who only recently had wed John Manning.

Among the assets going to Susan was a share of the profits from fabulously productive Houmas Plantation along the Mississippi River in Louisiana, where the Hamptons grew sugar cane with an army of nearly a thousand slaves. The old Hampton mansion at Houmas still stands and is open for tours (It's slightly provincial compared to Millford, but still handsome.). In any event, it seems highly likely Susan Hampton's newly inherited wealth from sugar cane built Millford (sugar cane prices were at their peak in 1840). In contrast, there is no record of any great agricultural effort on the sandy, hilly soil of Millford.

It seems to have been built purely as a pleasure dome in an exotic location (I'm reminded of Coleridge's "In Xanadu did Kubla Khan a stately pleasure dome decree." Sounds to me like Millford.). The house was built within two years of the death of Wade Hampton I, whose well-known frugality never would have countenanced such an extravagance as Millford. Susan and John Manning were both only twenty-two years of age at the time they commenced building Millford.

John Laurence Manning, however, was no *parvenu* dependent on the kindness and wealth of his Hampton in-laws. Descended from the Richardsons and Mannings, large landholders and politically powerful families in the Carolina midlands region, young Manning was the son of the then governor of South Carolina, Richard I. Manning, at the time of his engagement to the very eligible Miss Hampton. John Manning himself went on to become governor of South Carolina (1852-54) as did his son, Richard I. Manning II, after the Civil War.

The land on which Millford was built apparently had been given to Manning by his Richardson grandparents. Legend has it that when Manning was a youth, his grandfather offered him the chance to select a site from family lands for a future home. Millford is supposedly built on this site chosen by Manning as a youth.

(As a footnote to this chapter, my mother's great-grandfather was named Wade Malone Hampton, an Alabama cousin of the much richer South Carolina Wade Hampton, who had a brother, Richard Hampton.

The massive capitals of Millford's Corinthian columns make a classical backdrop for this marble bust of Diana by Hiram Powers.

By happenstance, I was named Richard Hampton in honor of my mother's grandfather. While a distant family relationship, it gives me one more tie to Millford. My father was also a native South Carolinian. Interestingly, one of the first of the original furnishings to come back to Millford after I bought the house was a portrait of Susan Hampton Manning, whose Hampton inheritance most likely built the place. A second portrait of Susan followed on the heels of the first. In most of my houses, it seems I have been able to establish some sort of personal connection to the previous owners.)

It is my opinion—mostly conjecture—that young Susan and John Manning were so bold as to embark, at age twenty-two, on building a home as extravagant as Millford largely because of encouragement from her older brother Wade Hampton II, whose generosity in tearing up his father's will made it possible for the Mannings to build it. Shortly after the completion of Millford, Wade Hampton II used the same architect-builder (Nathaniel Potter) to erect a similar residence—Millwood—for his own family on the site of Wade Hampton I's more modest home place nearer to Columbia. Wade Hampton II had been an investor in the Charleston Hotel, the prototype for both Millford and Millwood, and evidently was smitten by the monumental architectural style that Reichardt brought to Charleston from Europe. Millwood was burned in

Regal red hangings at the windows and a four-poster bed enliven this Millford bedroom. Barrytown Associates and Scalamandré created the classical carpet in brown with anthemion motifs. Virginia Pulver made all the curtains and bed hangings at Millford.

196

1865 by General Sherman (As its name suggests it was built of wood, unlike Millford, which is built entirely of brick, plaster, and granite.). But the six gigantic Corinthian columns of long-lost Millwood still stand today, a ghostly reminder of past glory. The Millwood columns have identical proportions to those at Millford.

Further supporting my thesis that Wade Hampton II was instrumental in influencing Susan and John Manning to go ahead and build such an elegant house at such a young age, we know that Hampton was a great connoisseur of the arts—the *beau ideal* of the pre-Civil War Southern Gentleman. Wade II, unlike his gruff self-made father, was well-read, well-traveled (throughout Europe), and a boon companion to local writers and artists, as well as being a great horseman and racing enthusiast. I'm sure Wade II encouraged this grand project for the greater glory of South Carolina and the baronial Hamptons.

While little is known of Susan Hampton Manning's tastes and aspirations, John Laurence Manning appears to have been cut from the same mold as his Hampton brother-in-law. He attended Princeton, and letters written to his parents indicate a keen sensibility. His father had given young John Laurence a letter of introduction to the governor of New Jersey, who resided in Princeton. A letter from John Laurence to his father describes how he absorbed the elegant style of life that was practiced by the governor of New Jersey. Among his observations, young Manning notes a heating furnace

My bedroom at Millford is mostly a restful blue comme d'habitude. The recamier couch by Phyfe is original to the house.

underneath the floor, unheard of in South Carolina at the time, supplementing the usual fireplace heating. Some years later Manning installed what has been described as the first central heating in South Carolina: a basement furnace under the central hall of Millford that suffused warm air throughout the house. It's still there, though no longer used. Clearly, the young southerner at Princeton was precocious and a keen observer. He also enthusiastically describes three courses of wines served in beautiful crystal by the governor of New Jersey at a candle-lit dinner, an early evidence of Manning's taste for the good life and a precursor to what must have been many gracious dinners in Millford's elegant dining room.

Susan Hampton Manning had only seven years of marriage before dying during the birth of her third child at her mother's home in Columbia. John Manning subsequently remarried Sally Bland Clarke from Virginia and there were four more children from this union. Until the eve of the Civil War, Millford continued as one of the focal points of power and society in South Carolina.

Visitors often ask how Millford survived the Civil War and how it escaped the fate of its near twin, Millwood, which was burned to the ground by Sherman. The answer seems to be that Northern troops did not reach Millford until April 19, 1865, in the final days of fighting. By some sort of divine providence, the troops that arrived at Millford were commanded by General Edward E. Potter. Governor Manning

What could be more evocative of the Old South than the tall Corinthian columns of Millford Plantation?

"welcomed him" at the front door and, on learning the general's name, is said to have observed "This house was built by a Potter and I suppose it will be destroyed by a Potter." The Northern general replied "No, you are protected." It seems General Potter was a relative of Nathaniel Potter, the architect-builder from Rhode Island who built Millford. Shortly thereafter, news was received at Millford of Lee's surrender to Grant at Appomattox on April 9th and the war's end. Millford was safe—though not from the coming depravities of Reconstruction and the long years of poverty that subsequently descended on South Carolina.

The Mannings managed to hang on to Millford into the early twentieth century. In 1902, a few years after Governor Manning's death, it was sold to Mary Clark Thompson, a wealthy New York widow of one of the original owners of the First National Bank of New York, the genesis of today's Citibank. Mrs. Thompson was instrumental in convincing her husband to back George Fisher Baker, who became, along with J.P. Morgan, the pre-eminent American banker of the later nineteenth and early twentieth centuries. Mrs. Thompson and George F. Baker had been friends since childhood and were said to have been romantically linked in later life after both were widowed. The fact that I owned Mr. Baker's house in New York at the time I bought Millford from Mary Thompson's family was one more example of the inter-connectedness of all my houses. Is this a family of souls moving through the years?

Mary Clark Thompson purchased Millford as a winter gathering place and hunting retreat for her family. Having no children of her own, she later willed the mansion to her Clark nephews who apparently were unrelated to Sally Bland Clarke, Governor Manning's

second wife. The Clarks totally refurbished Millford and gave it loving care for the next ninety years, delivering it from years of post-Civil War decay and neglect. Owned jointly in recent years by three different members of the Clark family, none of whom used it very frequently, Millford was sold to me in the spring of 1992. This was only the second change in ownership in more than 150 years—a sure sign to me that Millford was a place that one would become attached to. The Clarks, incidentally, still retain some 2,500 acres adjoining Millford, dwarfing my 400 acres, which include the old mansion. They still love the place and we all happily co-exist during holidays. Emory Clark's favorite log cabin from childhood days stands nearby, with huge fireplaces at either end of a lodge-like living room/dining room. He likes the fishing here, and I just like grand old houses, especially Millford.

Let me tell you about Millford today. Décor-wise it's actually a bit like going back to the beginning of this story, the days when the Mannings first built Millford.

In buying Millford from the Manning estate in 1902, "Aunt Mary" (Mary Clark Thompson) had insisted that most of the furnishings and contents remain as part of the sale. Thanks to her foresight, most of the original furniture was still at Millford when I bought the place. It's all documented through bills of sale, dated from 1840-43 from "D. Phyfe & Son," New York's most famous furniture maker, to Governor Manning. This furniture doesn't look at all like the earlier Federal-period furniture for which Duncan Phyfe is more renowned and which I own in other houses. The furniture at Millford represents a unique collection today of the final stylistic phase of Phyfe's furniture before his death in 1842. [For additional information on the large collection of late Phyfe furniture in Millford see Thomas Gordon Smith's article in the May 1997 issue of *The Magazine ANTIQUES*.]

Phyfe kept reinventing himself as styles changed—from the grandeur of Napoleonic Empire styling to the post-War of 1812 more populist Biedermeier-style furniture, made fashionable through the endless parties at the Treaty of Vienna following the defeat of Napoleon at Waterloo. Therefore, this late Phyfe furniture at Millford is both simpler (devoid of all ormolu, carving or stenciling) and sturdier; made for a more populist taste. Yet the lines are strictly classical, replicating the shapes of Greco-Roman furniture styles that were sweeping Europe at the time following the excavation of Roman ruins at Pompeii and Herculaneum.

The furniture I inherited at Millford had been stowed away in the attic, hallways, even the barn, in favor of the Clarks' English antiques. This original Manning furniture would have been only about sixty years old in 1902 when the Clarks bought the house, not old enough to qualify as antique but of an age to be

totally out of fashion. Most of this furniture had turned black with age and disuse by the time I came along. Suffice it to say that with a lot of cleaning and polishing, revealing the superb mahogany veneers Phyfe used, and new silk fabrics, this suite of furniture looks stunning back in its original setting. Also, with nearly 160 years of age, these pieces now qualify as bona fide antiques!

The interiors of Millford have been untouched structurally over the years. All of the original mahogany

(Left and above) Among the unusual outer buildings at Millford are the Greek Revival stables, the original plantation bell tower, and the Little Mansion, a guesthouse added by the Clarks in the 1920s.

doors, the silver locks, the marble mantels, the original plasterwork, even most of the original window panes with their wavy glass are still intact. Ceilings are very

(Left) This charming fountain statue of a little boy clutching a dolphin is original to the house and is the centerpiece of the formal garden outside the double parlors.

high—sixteen feet on the first floor and fourteen feet on the second—with huge floor-to-ceiling windows for ventilation and circulation in a hot climate.

One enters Millford through a sixteen-foot-wide central hall, traversing the house for nearly sixty feet from front to the grand circular staircase in the rear. The hall probably doubled as a ballroom. Because the Mannings were so young and so rich when the house was built, I have visions of fancy balls and endless entertainments at Millford. The enormous hallway was large enough to dance quadrilles, polkas, reels, waltzes and other energetic, fast dances which were all the rage at the time the house was built. Dancing in the front hall could have spilled over into the adjoining double parlors, which open *en suite* into one vast room. In fact, you could dance right out the giant windows onto the rear loggia or the front piazza if you were the romantic sort or were simply overheated from the exertion of dancing. Because of the remoteness of Millford, the Mannings' parties were said to commence in late afternoon, culminating in a midnight supper, with dancing continuing until dawn. Only then would it be safe for guests to return home by horse and carriage from Millford's remote location.

The most beautiful rooms at Millford are the high-ceilinged double parlors on the first floor. The parlors are divided by a screen of four tall Corinthian columns. The traditional sliding mahogany doors separating the two parlors are unusual in that they

(Above) The Porter's Lodge, at the original gates, gave visitors their first glimpse of Millford's classical architecture. (Below) My one new architectural contribution is a swimming pool, much needed in a hot climate, but out of sight from the main house.

fold back into the wall, revealing a mirrored exterior side. Indeed the entire suite is a veritable *palais de glace*; all windows and mirrors. Floor-to-ceiling mirrors are built into either end between the windows. Additional ceiling-high mirrors with simple gold frames are fitted above the two white marble mantels which were made in Philadelphia especially for Millford. The overall effect of so much fitted glass is almost art deco modern, but the mirrors are well documented as original, brought by ship from New York to Charleston in 1840 and then barged up the Santee River to Millford. How they survived such a long trek and nearly 160 years of usage is certainly a miracle. With a pair of circa 1840 Waterford chandeliers, which I have installed, the double parlors glitter with newfound glamour. Pale blue and gold carpets with a classical motif, designed by Bill Thompson and made by Scalamandré, and the original Phyfe furniture, reupholstered in blue and gold silk, complete the ensemble. This is certainly one of America's prettiest suites of rooms.

My personal favorite rooms, however, are on the other (west) side of the long central hall: a large dining room that is oval-shaped at one end, opening into a smaller, book-lined library. Both rooms have handsome crystal chandeliers hanging from the original plaster center medallions. I have the Mannings' oval-shaped long dining room table and fourteen original armchairs by Phyfe—unusually comfortable with arms on each that make you want to sit and chat and sip wine for hours by candlelight. Hanging over a pair of Phyfe marble-topped serving tables, made for the house, are portraits of Susan Hampton Manning and General Richard Richardson,

a Revolutionary War hero and grandfather of Governor Manning. The adjoining library is the least formal, most comfortable room in the house—with book-lined walls, a black marble mantel, and tall windows to the floor, showcasing vistas to the surrounding gardens. On chill winter evenings, the warm red carpets, curtains and a cheery fire in the black marble fireplace make this a cozy retreat.

Millford's second floor is almost as grand as the first. The most striking feature, as you ascend the stairs, is the handsome domed ceiling, with a stained glass oculus to emit light in the center, at the top of the rotunda enclosing the staircase. Going up and down the curving, winding staircase, made even more dramatic by red and gold carpet runners, reminds me of Hollywood's version of the grand staircase at Twelve Oaks in *Gone With the Wind*. Some said there was never such a grand staircase in the real Old South, but Millford's staircase proves there was. One can certainly make a grand entrance on this staircase, though it would have been hazardous with a hoop skirt.

From the top of the stairs, one faces another long hall, equally as wide as the entrance hall below. Here again, I have visions of children being taught to dance here, emulating their parents dancing below. There surely would have been a small orchestra or other musicians

The Spring House, a charming Gothic folly, built on a spring, is said to be a miniature version of Trinity Episcopal Church in Columbia, where the Mannings are buried. The delicious spring water that flows from this hillside, draped in wisteria and azaleas, gives new meaning to "Bourbon and branch water."

playing on the balcony overlooking the staircase. The cylindrical stairwell sweeps the music sounds all over the house. The balance of the second floor consists of four high-ceilinged bedrooms with marble fireplaces and baths and dressing closets in between. Above this floor is an attic floor with four more bedrooms but with much lower ceilings, only eight feet, presumably for children. Each of these attic bedrooms has a skylight, since the small side windows are like portholes, concealed within the acanthus leaf wreaths which ornament the exterior of Millford.

Aside from the mansion itself, there are some notable outer buildings that add to the charm and livability of the place. Directly behind the kitchen and laundry wings are a pair of smaller, two-bedroom cottages in matching Greek Revival architectural style, suggesting two small Grecian temples on either side of the rear courtyard. One of these belonged to "Daddy Ben," Governor Manning's faithful butler who remained alone to watch over deserted Millford after Governor Manning, in old age, had moved to Camden, South Carolina to live with his daughter. Daddy Ben's cottage—consisting of a small living room with a fireplace and a single bedroom—makes a perfect guest house today. The matching cottage opposite Daddy Ben's may have been built for the first Mrs. Manning's "Mammy," but it was long used as a garden house or potting shed by the Clarks. I now have it as another guest house.

Other original structures on the property include "Mammy Ann's Cottage" (she was the second Mrs. Manning's "Mammy," who came with her from Virginia). Located some distance from the main mansion, it was originally two rooms, like Daddy Ben's, but was expanded by the Clarks to include two more bedrooms and a kitchen. This has now been converted into a library. Directly behind the big mansion is a tall water tower/bell tower with the original plantation bell—the closest thing to a communications system on plantations of that era, summoning people to work, to quit work, to eat, etc. The tall cylindrical structure, which looks rather like a lighthouse, has a cistern concealed at the top which used to provide running water to the mansion, said to be the first such system in South Carolina. Just how the water got up there from a distant pond requires an understanding of something called a hydraulic ram, popular in the mid-nineteenth century, which literally forced the water up the hill through a leather pipe into the cistern at the top of the water tower. It then flowed by gravity into the mansion. Governor Manning clearly was thoroughly modern for his age!

Another charming original structure is the "Porter's Lodge," at the entrance gates to Millford. Also a Greek temple in form with two Ionic columns "in antis," this elegant little building provides the visitor with the first hint of the classical grandeur that is to come on arrival at the big mansion, up a sweeping circular drive. The gates to Millford also are original— in the then popular Egyptian style with six pylons supporting ornamental wrought-iron gates.

Completing the original ensemble of buildings is a very unusual and large Greek Revival barn and stables used for the Mannings' prized racehorses. I've never before seen stables designed to look like a Greek temple, but this one is, with six handsome fluted Doric columns along either side. The pediment contains a very decorative and large fan-like window (sometimes called a "Diocletian Window" after the Roman model), bringing light into the attic of the stables. It would be interesting for someone with more equestrian leanings than myself to restore the stables to their original state.

The Clark family's most notable addition to Millford is a guest house known as "The Little Mansion." Built in the 1920s about fifty yards to the rear of the big house, the Little Mansion completes the back side of the courtyard behind the mansion, flanked on the sides by the two guest houses. The Little Mansion is a well-executed simplified architectural mini-version of Millford, with a one-story four-column porch facing the mansion (my favorite shady area to sit and read a book and look up occasionally to admire the big house). The Little Mansion adds four more bedrooms, a living room and a kitchen to my capacity either for vast house parties in good times or a bed and breakfast if hard times come.

Aside from my restoration of the house, furniture and gardens, the reader might ask what has been my contribution to Millford? Answer: A swimming pool. This may not sound like much, but it goes a long way toward making life bearable during the warm months here. So mild is the winter climate at Millford, I've also used the pool (heated, of course) on mild days in January, February and March. It's a great addition to the good life at Millford.

Millford sits in pristine state today—my dream house with big columns on the hill, down south, overlooking acres of green lawn and moss-draped live oak trees. While I've only had use of it for the past six years since the restoration was complete, I've been surprised how much time I spend here. It's a great place for reading and writing. With thousands of

When dusk comes to Millford, the tall windows, brightly illuminated from within, become a "decorator's showcase" for promenades along the front piazza and loggia on the back side.

surrounding acres in swamp or park land, you are not disturbed by visitors or outdoor noise—only the sounds of nature, which are divine, especially at night when the bobwhite quail are calling and the frogs and crickets are singing. Because I view Millford as a national treasure (it is a registered National Historic Landmark), I try to share the house on occasion with museum groups, garden clubs, etc., even family reunions for the Richardsons, Mannings, Hamptons and Clarks. I've also had more house parties here than I ever would have expected in such a remote location. It's the perfect place to entertain. But I still haven't had one of those "dance till dawn" parties like the Hamptons used to give!

CHAPTER 15

HOME AWAY FROM HOME

This book would not be complete without some mention of all the collecting of Americana that I have done on behalf of Donaldson, Lufkin & Jenrette, the Wall Street investment banking house I helped co-found forty years ago, and—to a lesser extent—for The Equitable Life Assurance Society. The sheer quantity of portraiture of American business and political leaders, old prints, rare books and manuscripts, statuary and antique furnishings acquired for DLJ and Equitable over the years exceed what I have bought for my six houses. For me, at least, there was very little difference between being at home and at the office; both looked the same!

While I never bought any old houses for either DLJ or Equitable, I did recently entice AXA, the large French-based insurer which is now the largest shareholder in DLJ and Equitable, into buying a superb Greek Revival plantation—Berry Hill—in Virginia. Long unoccupied, Berry Hill, built in 1840, is being restored

For me, at least, there was very little difference between being at home and at the office; both looked the same.

Berry Hill Plantation, circa 1840, in Virginia.
No, I don't own it—but I did entice AXA into buying and restoring this spectacular Greek Revival mansion as a management training center.

and re-christened as a management training center in its new incarnation. Having observed AXA meticulously restore several old chateaux and vineyards in France, I am confident that they will bring sensitivity to Berry Hill's restoration. The house also is well protected by easements given to the state of Virginia.

My hobby of collecting antiques has been very much intertwined with my business career. About twenty-five years ago, when I became chief executive officer of Donaldson, Lufkin & Jenrette, I decided our firm—which was then one of the youngest on Wall Street—could use the cachet of antiquity. Perhaps I was secretly trying to clone Brown Brothers Harriman & Co., my Freudian first experience on Wall Street. After some of the terrible days in the stock market in the 1970s, which everyone now seems to have forgotten, I felt that DLJ's offices should reflect stability and continuity, as well as the quality look that the portraits of financial leaders from yore, antiques, and other *objets d'art* imparted to our quarters. I also felt that these acquisitions would be much better investments than buying all new office furnishings that typically have no resale value. It seemed to work. Our clients liked the

Dan Lufkin's favorite American Whaling Scene, *circa 1840, with its patriotic overtones, still dominates the DLJ Board Room. Also shown is DLJ's George Washington Clock by Du Buc, Paris.*

(Right) DLJ created this elegant double staircase to showcase the firm's prize portrait of Alexander Hamilton by John Trumbull. The bust is also of Hamilton, by Horatio Stone. To the right at the top of the stairs is a portrait of Secretary of Treasury Andrew Mellon.

distinctive Americana look, and the firm is very much alive and well today—unlike most other firms started at that time which have long since disappeared.

Without doubt, DLJ has the finest and most extensive collection of Americana of any bank or investment bank on Wall Street or anywhere else. Indeed, I can think of no other company in any industry that has anything comparable. Brown Brothers Harriman & Co. probably comes closest (its collection documents the firm's remarkable 182-year history). Yet in buying and assembling DLJ's collection we never reached or paid top prices. Most of these things were acquired when Americana was out of favor in the 1970s.

Contrary to conventional wisdom, I didn't start DLJ's collection. The seminal credit goes to Dan Lufkin, one of our co-founders, who made the first purchase—thereby shocking us all! DLJ was started with $100,000 equity capital (plus some borrowed funds) in December 1959. Some years later, Lufkin walked in with a large painting (nearly eight feet wide!) of an American whaling scene, circa 1840, which he had bought for DLJ. Its most striking feature was a huge American flag, patriotically draped over half of the painting. The other half depicted whalers harpooning a whale, gushing blood; a rather grisly scene. The artist was unknown. When Dan told us he had paid $30,000 for the painting (it seemed like a lot more money then), we were aghast; that was 30% of our initial equity capital in DLJ! In Dan's defense, DLJ had become quite profitable by then, so the purchase was not as extravagant as it might seem relative to our starting net worth. It makes an amusing story in hindsight. The last time we had *The American Whaling Scene* painting appraised, it was said to be worth nearly $300,000. It now hangs proudly in DLJ's boardroom. Dan was so proud of it he had Robert Jackson paint a copy for his home.

From the DLJ old print and manuscript collection:

(Above left) Federal Hall in New York City served briefly as the nation's capitol. George Washington took the oath of office from the balcony.

(Middle) Currier & Ives Life in the Woods, *"Returning to Camp," 1860.*

(Below) Letter from Alexander Hamilton to the Bank of New York, dated 1790, authorizing disbursement of $20,000.

DLJ's next foray into antiquities was attributable to Richard Hexter, now deceased and one of the most brilliant people ever to join DLJ. In 1966, Dick became persuaded that old letters and manuscripts relating to the financing of the American Revolution would go sky-high in value by 1976—the 200th Anniversary of the American Revolution. So we quietly began to buy old letters and other manuscripts, especially those signed by or written to Alexander Hamilton and Robert Morris, the two chief financial architects of the early American republic. We also sought out letters signed by Washington, Jefferson and other Revolutionary War leaders relating to how the war was financed. Our collection sought to document not only how the American Revolution was financed, but also how New York City emerged as the financial center of the nation. Today, we literally have thousands of these important letters and manuscripts, and they are enormously valuable, not only financially, but to scholars. Hexter's thesis that America's Bicentennial would produce a bull market in these manuscripts was right on. But Dick also predicted we would "fall in love" with the collection and never sell. So far, he's been right.

(Above) John Trumbull painted Alexander Hamilton while he was the nation's first Secretary of the Treasury. DLJ's large collection of manuscripts from Hamilton's era are a fitting complement to the portrait.

(Below) Gilbert Stuart painted 70 copies of his so-called Atheneum-style portrait of George Washington. DLJ's is said to be one of the best. The mirror image of this portrait appears on the one-dollar bill.

Equitable's neo-classical board room provided a perfect setting for some of the portraits of members of the Chamber of Commerce who also had been Equitable directors.

Two other major additions to DLJ's collection of Americana came from acquisitions. In 1977, DLJ acquired two old-line Wall Street firms: Pershing & Company and Wood, Struthers & Winthrop. Jack Pershing, son of the famous World War I general and founder of the firm, had collected *hundreds* of prints of old New York scenes from the first half of the nineteenth century, including many views of Wall Street in its early days. I was told that he bought them during the Depression 1930s when they were practically given away (which is about what we paid for them in buying

Pershing at book value). Wood, Struthers & Winthrop, which manages money for high-net-worth individuals, also had a superb collection of Currier & Ives lithographs of American scenes, in mint condition, from the mid-nineteenth century. They are still with us in WSW's quarters at 277 Park Avenue. When times

The dining room at Equitable is dominated by a full-length portrait of Cadwallader Colden, the last British colonial governor of New York. He seems overwhelmed by the massive gilt American eagle, all original to the Chamber of Commerce collection, as are the other portraits.

are bad in the market, they send a soothing message to clients that "we've been around a long time and this too shall pass."

Other than these two important additions to DLJ's collection that came with companies that we acquired, I can claim responsibility for most of the other major acquisitions up until the time of my retirement. We made a "quantum leap" in 1983, when I heard via the grapevine that the New York Chamber of Commerce planned to sell its baronial hall on Wall Street and move uptown to sleek modern quarters (with low ceilings, not very good for displaying large portraits). This meant they had no really satisfactory place to install some 350 portraits of New York and other American business and political leaders that adorned

The Atlantic Cable Projectors, *by Daniel Huntington,*
is my favorite painting from the Chamber of Commerce
collection. Cyrus W. Field, on right in elegant house
coat, had been an Equitable Director before leading
a consortium of investors that financed the underwater
cable across the Atlantic, opening up modern
high-speed communication.

the Chamber's Great Hall near Wall Street. The decision was made to sell the portraits (I was not a member of the Chamber and not part of that decision), and they were appraised by a New York art dealer, who established a price for each.

By sheer good luck, I arrived precisely at the time prices were established and the entire collection went on the block. I would have liked to have bought the whole collection (the prices seemed reasonable), but I felt our firm was still too poor and we did not have enough space for the whole collection (I was not deterred by the low ceilings of our offices.). So I set up two simple criteria to determine what to buy: 1. the

subject of the portrait had to have stood the test of time; or 2. the *artist* had to have stood the test of time. Some of the portraits, of course, met both criteria. Following these criteria, I bought fifty of the portraits for DLJ. The two most important, by far, were a life-sized, full-length portrait of Alexander Hamilton by John Trumbull, and an "Atheneum"-style portrait of George Washington by Gilbert Stuart (the mirror image is found on the dollar bill). While my credentials to judge art might be questioned, I personally believe the regal, life-sized painting of Alexander Hamilton is John Trumbull's finest work. Yale, which has much of Trumbull's work, would kill to get it, as would the U.S. Treasury. It was painted in 1792 while Hamilton served as the nation's first Secretary of the Treasury, and was a gift to the Chamber paid for by contributions from prominent citizens of New York City.

But the saga of the Chamber of Commerce portraits did not end with this sale to DLJ. The remaining portraits were not sold, for reasons unknown to me, perhaps because we had skimmed the cream and the rest were considered uninteresting (at least at that time). Years later, when I was chairman of The Equitable, we were able to obtain all the remaining portraits, which had been seemingly unloved and uncared for, stored out of sight in the attic of the New York Historical Society. The Historical Society's attic leaked and the portraits were at risk. *The New York Times* did an expose on the damage, and I seized the moment to offer to buy them all for Equitable. This time the Chamber declined to sell, but agreed instead to put them on permanent loan in return for Equitable's agreement to clean, restore and display them.

As a result, between DLJ and Equitable we have kept intact virtually the entire remarkable collection of the New York Chamber of Commerce portraits. The collection is a veritable history of American business, from colonial times up through the Depression of the 1930s when the Chamber seemed to give up adding new portraits. Not one is a woman, which doesn't thrill DLJ's growing ranks of women executives, but times they are a-changing!

All these portraits, prints and manuscripts at DLJ are now displayed against an appropriate background of draperies and period furnishings, designed originally by Edward Vason Jones, in association with David Byers. More recently, Mark Hampton supervised DLJ's move from the Wall Street area to new offices at 277 Park Avenue. He retained the Federal-period look, recycling many of the original draperies, wall papers, carpets, antiques and other furnishings that Ed Jones had selected for us in the 1970s.

Now that I'm retired, the caretakers of the collection at DLJ are two heroines: Margize Howell and Kathy Healy. They have been fully supported by John Chalsty and Joe Roby, past and present CEOs of DLJ. Margize and Kathy have devotedly maintained and expanded the collection (Pari Stave has done an equally terrific job as the guardian angel of Equitable's collection and art gallery, backed by my successors Joe Melone and Ed Miller.). Thanks to their efforts, DLJ's numerous new offices around the world all have the same American Federal Empire look as our New York home office. I suppose there are those who feel this look is old fashioned, but it is timeless, standing the test of time for DLJ for nearly forty years. It is surely a hidden asset on the firm's balance sheet.

Alliance Capital Management somehow escaped my Federal-period yoke when it was separated from DLJ after the sale to Equitable and came under the leadership of Dave Williams. But Dave and his wife, Reba White Williams, clearly are infected by the same collecting bug that bit me, perhaps even more so. Alliance's offices are festooned with thousands of rare and valuable prints by American print-makers of the *twentieth* century. The look is totally different from DLJ and bears the stamp of these two dedicated collectors. Between DLJ and Alliance, we have the art and business history of the past two centuries well covered.

It has been forty-two years since Mrs. Yorke induced me to buy my first antique and thirty-two years since I bought my first old house—the Roper House. After so many years of collecting (described in numerous magazine articles) and various awards related to my preservation activities, it seems that old houses and antiques have become my *persona*. This identity apparently has superseded my forty-year career on Wall Street, which included founding and nurturing some very successful firms (DLJ, Alliance) and rescuing The Equitable from the financial brink. All are now doing extremely well without me—which pleases me enormously. That I should now be better known for restoring old houses and antiques comes as something of a surprise to me. Perhaps the answer is that there are so many success stories on Wall Street these days that former achievements in a more difficult environment quickly pale or are forgotten in comparison with the vast sums that have been made in recent years. *Sic transit gloria!*

On the other hand, it seems to be far more distinctive to have domain over so many fine old houses and antiques. I don't have much competition in this department. That, of course, was *not* the reason I bought any of these wonderful old houses. Each seemed to me worth saving, not only for posterity but because I fell in love with the houses. I hope this book will encourage new converts to the joys of owning, restoring and loving old houses.

No, this is not a scene from "On Golden Pond," but it is my favorite spot at Edgewater to watch sunsets, reflect on the past, think about the future and—most of all— enjoy the present.

INDEX

PHOTO CREDITS

We are grateful to the following photographers and publications for permission to use their photographs:

Bill Aller, pages 29, 30, 31, 34-35, 36-37, 39, 40

Douglas Baz, page 10

Tria Giovan, page 144

John M. Hall (courtesy of Architectural Digest*), pages 146-147, 152, 155 small, 158, 159, 160, 166, 170-171, 172, 174*

John M. Hall (courtesy of Veranda*), pages 200, 202, 205 bottom*

François Halard (courtesy of GQ*), page 51*

Van Jones Martin, pages 56, 176-177, 180-181, 182 top, 183, 185 small, 186, 188, 193, 198-199, 204

Robert Philips, page 48

Paul Rocheleau (courtesy of The Magazine ANTIQUES*), pages 14, 17, 20, 80, 84, 104, 209*

Peter Vitale, page 76

David Turner (courtesy of W Magazine*), page 6*

Dorothy Zeidman, pages 216, 217

All other photographs by John M. Hall or used with permission of the owners.